Good News Club Series

Captives in the Wilderness

by Kathryn Dahlstrom

Good News Clubs®,
weekday Bible clubs for boys and girls,
are sponsored by
Child Evangelism Fellowship® Inc.

Published by

CEF PRESS®
P. O. Box 348
Warrenton, MO 63383-0348

ISBN 1-55976-828-2

1

Carlos felt absolutely frantic. They were going to miss the bus! He'd looked forward to this trip for weeks, but they'd wind up stuck at home unless his sister *hurried*.

"Anna!" (pronounced AH-nuh) he yelled. "What are you *doing?* Taking the whole house? We gotta *go!"*

Anna's voice carried from the girls' bedroom. It sounded muffled, like she had her head stuck in a drawer. Or the closet, maybe. "I know, I know! I'm coming as quick as I can, really!"

"The bus leaves in ten minutes!" He began to sway from foot to foot. "It'll take us at least five to walk to the meeting place!"

"I know, I know!" Her voice lowered until he couldn't make out her words, but he could tell she was speaking rapidly to someone. He pursed his lips and watched Maria

and Victoria, in kindergarten and second grade, gallop out
of the bedroom on some urgent errand for their thirteen-
year-old sister. They adored Anna and did whatever she
asked without question.

Why won't they run their tails off for me? Carlos wondered in irritation. Probably because Anna was too kind to
take advantage of them. Probably because he wasn't a teen-
ager yet—he was eleven years old—and went to the same
elementary school they did. And probably because he liked
to tease them. Doesn't every older brother do that, though?

He leaned against the living room wall as Maria
scampered down the narrow hallway and skidded through
the kitchen door. She shouted in Spanish, *"Mama!* Anna
can't find her favorite sweater!"

Mama, who spoke little English, looked up from
diapering Rosa, the youngest member of the Hernandez
family. "Eh? I just washed it," she answered in the same
language her daughter was using. "It should be with her
other clothes." Maria started to race back to Anna. But
Carlos blocked her way with a scowl.

"Tell her to skip it, you know? This is getting
ridiculous! Better yet, tell her I'm going without her!" He

2

backed up enough to let Maria slip past him with a wide-eyed stare, then grabbed his rolled-up blankets and pillow with one hand and his battered suitcase and lunch sack with the other. *Girls! Why did she wait 'til this morning to pack? Why couldn't she have done it last night?*

The suitcase handle wobbled dangerously as he marched toward the door. He hoped it wouldn't pull loose. He and his fifteen-year-old brother, Luis, had found the worn-out old case in the garage. The handle dangled on one remaining screw and its clasps no longer worked. But Carlos decided to fix it. Anything was better than carrying his clothes and towels and soap in plastic grocery bags.

He and Luis used thick wrappings of silver duct tape to secure the handle. They tied the case shut with a piece of twine. Their repair job worked well until Carlos loaded it with stuff. Now he wasn't so sure.

But he was too excited about the trip to let a gimpy suitcase bother him. He and Anna were members of a Good News Club. The older club kids were about to join dozens of other inner-city children for a week at a Bible camp near Yosemite National Park. Carlos had never seen wilderness before, and he could hardly wait. That is, if they didn't miss the *bus* . . . .

"Anna!" He glared through the doorway at the kitchen clock. *Four minutes to nine!* The bus was scheduled to *leave* at nine! He dropped his suitcase and yanked open the front door.

"Wait!" chorused two female voices. Mama and Anna raced toward him. His older sister had her arms full of bags and bundles and Mama's were wide open. She crushed Carlos in a hug (her hands smelled like baby wipes), smacked Anna on the cheek with her lips, and shooed them out the door.

They ran as fast as their stuff would let them, waving over their shoulders at Maria and Victoria, who shouted from the doorway, "Bye, you guys," and, "I wish *we* could go." Eager barks from the backyard followed them, too. "See you in a week, Peppy!" Carlos called. He missed his golden retriever already.

But there was precious little time to dwell on feelings. *Two minutes to nine!*

His suitcase jerked ominously and he thought he could see the tape stretching as he jogged along. "Hold on, you!" he ordered the handle.

"What?" gasped Anna. She was fighting to keep her blanket from unrolling and one of her plastic bags was getting a tear in it.

"Nothing. Just talking to my suitcase."

She started to laugh but wound up panting. They were both running out of breath. "Let's slow down!"

"We can't!" In spite of the never-ending roars and squeals and rattles of passing traffic, he thought he heard a diesel engine starting up.

They rounded the last corner. To Carlos' total relief, the bus was still there! A long line of kids stood beside it. A silvery-blond lady caught sight of them and waved them on. "*Hustle,* you two!" shouted Mrs. Peterson, one of the Good News Club leaders. "They're almost ready to leave!"

Carlos felt his cheeks turn red, from more than just exertion. Anna suddenly gave a scream and stopped running. One of her plastic bags ripped apart and brushes, barrettes, makeup and soap scattered over the grimy sidewalk. He whirled around to help her, disgusted at the delay and at the prospect of picking things up off concrete that was covered with ice cream splotches and squashed chewing gum, once white or pink or mint green and now pitch black.

As he grabbed and stuffed the runaway things in her other bags, Carlos glanced at the bus. *Oh, great!* The other kids were placing their gear in the outside luggage compartment. Soon they'd be loaded up and waiting impatiently for them. *How embarrassing!*

But then Carlos saw two older kids break away from the line and run toward them. Felipe (pronounced Fay-LEEP) and Mashell (pronounced Muh-SHELL)! Good friends....

Anna was nearly in tears as she pawed under a scraggly evergreen bush near an alley fence. "I'm still missing my *toothbrush!* And some lipstick, I think!"

Mashell dropped down beside her and felt under the bush. "Don't you just hate it when this stuff happens, girlfriend? Hold on! I think I got somethin'!" She pulled her hand out from under the bush; her deep brown fingers were wrapped around a gold tube.

"Yeah! That's it!" said Anna in relief. "But now where's my toothbrush?"

"I stuck it in one of your bags!" Carlos couldn't have kept disgust out of his voice if he'd wanted to. He shook his head at Felipe. "Girls!"

"Okay! Here it is!" sang out Anna. "You were right, Carlos. Thanks for the help."

He grabbed his suitcase without answering and ran toward the bus. But now it was his turn to be humbled. He reached the line as the last two kids shoved their gear into the bus's storage bin. He caught a glimpse of a long, black portable radio at a boy's feet. Then his suitcase handle suddenly broke free and the case thunked to the ground, skidded along the sidewalk and smashed into the radio.

"Watch it!" yelled the kid. "That's my boom box!" His name was Nathaniel Bronson and he was in Mashell's sixth-grade class. Everyone called him Bronce; he was known for his easy-going, friendly personality. But he wasn't acting that way now.

Not that anyone could blame him for getting upset. Carlos' case wound up rocking on top of the boom box like a teeter-totter on a block. Bronce reached it first, upended the suitcase and let it slam down like a toppled building. He snatched up his radio and held it to his chest as though it was an injured baby.

"Hey, man, I'm really sorry about your boom box.
See, my stupid handle—" Carlos started to mumble.
But Bronce cut him off with a near-scream.

"Just stay away from it! You got that? Leave it alone!
And while you at it, keep away from *me!* You a *menace!*"

Carlos stared at him. Bronce was breathing like
someone about to have a heart attack. He was still clutching
the radio with a knuckle-stretching grip and his eyes had the
fear of a wild animal in them.

Mashell strolled up to him. "Hey, Bronce, what you
gettin' all upset for? Carlos just had a accident, that's all.
He didn't mean for his handle to break. Your radio got a
little scratched maybe, but I bet it still works."

Before he could stop her, she reached for the radio/tape
switch and flicked it up. The only sound the boom box
made was a hollow click. He pulled away from her with his
empty hand clenched in a fist. *"Don't touch it!"*

Mashell raised one eyebrow at him. "Chill *out.* I'm just
tryin' to help. How come we ain't hearin' no tunes? Did it
really get busted up? Lemme see...."

"NO!" Sweat was filling the creases of his brown
forehead. Kids hopped off the bus and stared at him. Mrs.
Peterson spoke up. "What's wrong, Nathaniel?"

Anna explained what happened. "Would you like me to try and fix it?" offered the lady with a flick of her hand through her short curls. "I'm pretty good at jury-rigging things." She gave her watch an impatient glance. "I might as well do *something* while we're waiting for two of your adult counselors to get here."

"No, please! I—it's—not broken, really," stammered Bronce. "I—I—don't got any batteries in it, that's all. It's fine. I know it is."

A boy in the growing crowd of children pulled a package from a backpack. "Here! I got some batteries you can use."

Mrs. Peterson beamed. "That's very generous of you, Tony."

Nathaniel Bronson looked more and more like a terrified creature caught in a trap. "No—thanks. I just wanna leave my radio alone. And—you know, let it rest."

"Why don't you test it to see if it *works?*" argued Mashell.

"Why don't you get your nose outta my *business?*" Bronce looked like he was ready to start a fist fight. But the whole group was suddenly distracted by two adults loping toward them, red-faced, with hair flying and suitcases dragging. Carlos knew them well. The Good News Club's youngest leader, Miss Becky Lindstrom, and her boyfriend Stan. They were in their twenties. And they were going along as camp counselors. They reached the group, clutched their sides and sucked in air.

"We're *so sorry!*" panted Stan. "My Great Dane, Charlie, did *not* want to be left at the dog kennel . . . ."

"No need to explain," said Mrs. Peterson patiently. "Why don't you take time to breathe while we finish loading everything in the bus . . . ."

Ten minutes later they were on the move at last, and not too soon for Carlos. The kids waved through the windows at Mrs. Peterson, who disappeared as the bus rumbled around a corner. He couldn't *wait* to leave the smoggy air and dingy streets and graffiti-covered walls of Los Angeles behind. He'd seen pictures of woods and lakes and pine-covered mountains. But he couldn't imagine what they were like for real.

Everyone seemed as excited as he was. Chattering, laughing, squealing. Everyone except Bronce, who sat by himself with his precious radio beside him, one hand resting on it.

Carlos was mystified. He'd never seen anyone throw such a fit over a *thing*. Even more puzzling, if the boom box meant that much to Bronce, why wouldn't he let anyone fix it? What good was a *silent* radio?

Well, he wasn't going to dwell on it. He wasn't about to let *anything* bother him. This promised to be the best week of his life. And certainly the most exciting.

Mashell's head nodded and drowsiness fogged over her. That is, until she felt a jab in her ribs. "Look who's asleep!" Felipe whispered. "Now's our chance!"

She was wide awake in an instant, which couldn't be said for the rest of the kids. They'd been swaying along in the bus for *hours* through country that was sort-of interesting at first, but it got boring in a hurry. Camel-colored dirt. Straw-brown grass. Everything covered with dust. Orange groves that gave the land *some* green—except the trees, in straight rows, were much shorter and stumpier than she thought they'd be.

She liked catching sight of oranges and lemons hanging heavy on the branches. But that got boring too. So did singing and yelling and telling jokes and chatting with Anna about clothes and hairstyles . . . .

They ate sack lunches at a rest stop picnic area, then got
back in the bus long before Mashell was ready to sit still
again. As the kids around them fell asleep one by one, she
and Carlos and Felipe got to planning, in whispers, what
they'd do to Bronce if he nodded off. Hide his radio, of
course. This guy needed to *lighten up*.

And Felipe was right. Now was their chance. Bronce's
head rocked forward, then back, then rested sideways on the
seat back. His limp hand fell off the boom box. "Lemme
do it," Mashell breathed.

Anna dozed beside her. Best not to wake her or she'd
try to stop them. Mashell edged off her seat with a wary
glance at Miss Lindstrom and Stan, who were both asleep.
In fact, Stan was snoring.

Mashell swung herself across the aisle to the seat behind
Bronce. So far so good. She leaned over his seat back and
rested her chin on it until an extra hard jounce drove her
teeth into her tongue. *Ow! Girl, you got oatmeal for
brains? Watch yourself!*

She took a deep breath, reached her arm over and
touched the radio's black handle. Slowly, gingerly, she
lifted the handle to its upright position, then—*oh, boy!*—

lifted the radio off the seat. Then over the seat back. Then
onto her lap.

Hoo! She got it! Carlos and Felipe gave her a silent
cheer. Now for phase two. Eight-year-old Tony had been
the first to drop off. He was curled in a ball with his head
resting on his folded jacket. His rolled-up sleeping bag sat
under the seat. He insisted on bringing it inside the bus
rather than shoving it in the outside storage bin. Lucky
for them.

Mashell gave the radio to Felipe, then crawled down the
aisle and under Tony's seat. She hugged the bag to her
chest for the return trip. It didn't take them long to wrap the
radio inside. Mashell put it back under Tony's seat and the
three conspirators wound up sitting in their normal places
with halos over their heads.

It was all Mashell could do to keep from waking Bronce.

The scenery grew more interesting. They'd been rolling
between round-topped hills dotted with squat, bushy trees.
But now the bus labored up a winding, steep-sided
mountain grade. Mashell stared out her window with a
thumping heart. Kids on the other side of the bus saw thick
woods mixed with pines and tall, leafy trees. But she

looked out at clear, blue, sky and nothing but a metal
guardrail between the bus and a three-thousand-foot drop.
It took all her courage to peer at the valley far below, with
trees that she knew were full-grown but looked like bottle
brushes and moss clumps from this height.

*Lord, please help the driver keep this bus in control! We
ain't no airplane!* the girl prayed.

In spite of her nervousness, she liked what she saw.
Soon the valley was cut off by layer after layer of forest-
covered mountains spreading out all around her. She'd seen
desert mountains before—rugged, dry and covered with
scruffy bushes. But this range was so lush that everything
looked green except boulders and tree trunks. And even
they had moss on them. She'd never seen so much green in
her life.

Most of the kids were awake now and admiring the
scenery too. Excited chatter filled the bus. Suddenly a
furious voice cut through the talk. "All right! Where is it!"
Bronce stood and gripped the seat back in front of him as
the bus rounded a sharp curve. He glowered at the other
young passengers. "Give it back or I'll break your legs!"

"Sit down, Nathaniel," said Stan.

"So help me, I'm gonna bust up the guy who's got it!"

"Sit down before you get hurt."

Bronce obeyed reluctantly, forming both hands into tight fists.

Mashell glanced at Carlos and Felipe, which was a mistake. When she realized they were fighting as hard as she was not to laugh, she—and the other two—lost the battle. Giggles burst out of them like water from a tight, full hose.

"Give it *back,* Hernandez!" shouted Bronce. "One of you has it!"

Carlos spread his hands and looked innocent. "No we don't. Really! Check our stuff...."

Bronce would have done so in an instant if Stan hadn't stood and blocked him from getting up. "No children are allowed out of their seats when the bus is mo—*ving!*" The bus lurched and the young man lost his balance as if to prove his point. He nearly plopped into Bronce's lap. Which made Mashell laugh even harder.

Stan sat beside Bronce and continued to speak with all the dignity he could muster. "Now, what's the source of the conflict here?"

The sixth-grade boy let him know in no uncertain terms. "Whoever has the radio, give it back," said Stan.

"Now, please."

No one moved, which drew a frown from the young man. "Carlos, Felipe, Mashell—must you be deprived of camp privileges?" put in Miss Lindstrom sternly.

"We don't got it!" insisted Mashell. But she couldn't keep her lips from twitching.

There was a gasp from Tony, who had reached for his sleeping bag. He unrolled it, then held up the radio with utter surprise on his face.

"To-NEE!" yelled the three conspirators. Mashell continued, "Ooh, you in trouble now!"

The eight year old turned pale. "But, but I didn't . . . ."

Bronce never let him finish his sentence. "Give it *back* you little crumb snatcher!" He shot past Stan, grabbed the boom box and shoved Tony sideways—so hard that his head slammed against the window. The younger boy gripped his right ear and let out a wail of pain as blood trickled down his arm.

Miss Lindstrom was at his side in a second, holding him with one arm and fumbling through a backpack with the

other. Anna rushed forward and helped her pull out first-aid
supplies—antiseptic towelettes, ointment, bandages.
Meanwhile, Stan rose to his feet and anger came out in his
voice. "Get back in your seat, Nathaniel! This is not a
boxing ring. I will *not* have anyone getting hurt!"

Bronce sat down sullenly, still clutching his boom box.
Stan turned to Carlos, Felipe and Mashell. "You planted
that radio in Tony's sleeping bag, didn't you?"

"We was just tryin' to get Bronce to lighten up,"
explained Mashell. "We didn't think he'd shove anybody
around." She gave her classmate a questioning look.
"What'd you go and push Tony for? We didn't want
nobody gettin' *hurt.*"

Bronce didn't answer her. "Is his ear okay?" asked Carlos
in a worried voice. "Does he need stitches or something?"

Miss Lindstrom wiped her hands with a tissue. "No, he
should be fine. It's just a little cut. Right, Tony?" Tony
nodded and she mashed him in a sideways hug. "But this
should be a lesson to all of you. What you thought was a
harmless joke got someone injured."

"Bronce," added Stan, "I think you owe someone an
apology."

Bronce stared straight ahead and spoke in a tight voice. "I'm sorry you got hurt, Tony. I didn't mean to push you so hard."

"You shouldn't have pushed him at all! I want to talk to you and Carlos and Felipe and Mashell as soon as we get there. I wouldn't be surprised if the camp has some chores that need doing." Stan stood and staggered back to his place beside Miss Lindstrom. Silence overshadowed the bus's engine rumbles and the creaks and squeaks and rattles of its seats and windows.

Mashell rolled her eyes at her fellow radio-nappers. "Wonder what they gonna make us do?" she whispered. "Peel potatoes?"

Felipe moaned. "Maybe we'll have to clean toilets!"

So much for their bright idea. What a way to start a week of Bible camp! She stole a look at Bronce, who was sitting like a statue, clutching the radio and looking like he was going to explode.

What was *with* him, anyway?

* * * * * * *

They were ordered to sweep out the guest cabins after supper, when everyone else had an hour of free time. Bad enough, but the punishment could have been worse. Now that he knew what he faced, Carlos could forget it and enjoy himself.

He couldn't imagine feeling cranky in a place like this. His eyes feasted on cracked-bark pine trees—as tall as skyscrapers, he imagined. And green grass everywhere, only it wasn't mowed short except around the cabins. It came nearly to his waist and had lacy seeds on top. Wild flowers with tiny purple or yellow or white blossoms were mixed in. He kept sniffing hard just to absorb all the tangy-pine and sweet-flower and green-growing smells. Not a trace of oil refinery sulfur or car fumes.

But the lake was his favorite sight. Half a mile wide and two miles long, it was surrounded by pines on a shore-line of silver granite slabs and gravel. Sunlight twinkled like a million diamonds on its surface and its water was so clear that he could see rocks and seaweed and fish swimming easily through underwater sun patches.

The place had a logical name: Pine Lake Bible Camp. *One week isn't enough,* Carlos decided. *I'm coming back next year!*

The camp director, Mr. Tom Hansen, called the young campers together, forty in all. They sat cross-legged on the ground in a large clearing facing the lake and he gave them camp rules in a commanding voice. "Above all," he told them, "keep food out of your tents. This is bear country and any snack, no matter how tightly wrapped you think it is, could draw a hungry black bear to you. Would you like that?"

Nervous chuckles and murmers of "No way!" filtered through the group. "Therefore, lock all your food and soaps and toothpaste and anything else with a strong odor in the food lockers."

He pointed to several large metal boxes, about the size of furniture crates and painted chocolate brown, placed around the outside of the clearing. Carlos craned his neck to see them. They looked strong. Impossible for a bear to get into. Which was probably a good thing.

But he couldn't resist leaning close to Felipe and whispering, "I'd like to see a big old black bear face to face. Wouldn't that be *cool?*"

Felipe gave him a you-must-be-crazy look. "Only if I was looking at him through a window and I was *inside.*"

Next, tents. The boys were to camp in this clearing and the girls in a meadow across the stream that chattered its way toward the lake. The group split up and everyone tackled the job of putting up the two-sleeper pup tents.

Mr. Hansen explained how, of course. Then he offered a prize to the pair of kids that got their tent up first. Carlos and Felipe pounced on theirs. But the nylon tent, when unrolled, turned into a rumpled mess with colored loops that were supposed to match the poles, if they could only get the poles put together. They stared in confusion at the tangled aluminum sticks. How were they ever going to get them long and straight?

They twisted and yanked and argued with each other until a boy setting up his tent next to theirs showed them that each pole was a thin, hollow tube with elastic cord folded into short lengths running through it. "All you gotta do," he said, "is bend each piece out straight, then pull on it 'til you see the elastic. Then you let go and the elastic snaps it into the next piece and it keeps getting longer and longer. See?"

Carlos was getting cranky. "Thanks!" he snarled.

Fitting the poles into the loops didn't work much better. The first pole they tried snagged somewhere in the fabric.

Carlos tried another and the same thing happened.

"You're supposed to use the red-tipped pole," insisted Felipe. "Red pole for red *loops!*"

"But it won't *go!*"

"Yes it will," said the kid next door. "You just gotta jiggle it."

Carlos glared at him. "I tried jiggling and pulling and pushing and *kicking!* What do you gotta do to get these things to *work?*"

The kid did it for them, and the pole slid easily into place, of course. Everything worked well for him and his partner. In fact, they won the "fastest tent maker" prizes—two brand-new compasses. The kid, whose name was Scott, proudly showed his to Carlos. "My dad and I go camping a lot."

"You might know we'd get Daniel Boone for a neighbor," Carlos muttered to Felipe. They wound up last, to add insult to injury.

Supper greatly improved his mood. Hamburgers grilled over fire grates. He sat between Felipe and Scott at a picnic table with long, attached benches on each side and wood that was unvarnished and gray. He'd taken to calling Scott "Daniel Boone" but Scott didn't seem to mind. The boys ate and watched the sun sink until its light turned everything amber and the lake looked like polished copper.

Stan strolled toward them as Carlos finished off a chocolate chip cookie. Mashell and Bronce walked beside him with Mashell talking a mile a minute and Bronce looking sulky. Oh, yeah. Floor sweeping.

The four kids followed their leader to a row of two-room log cabins near the edge of the woods. "Have at it," said Stan, pointing to four brooms and dustpans lined up against the first one's front door. "If you work quickly, you won't miss any campfire time. But do a good job. I'm going to inspect your work."

Bronce grabbed a broom and stomped off to the second cabin without a word. "Nothing like teamwork," said Mashell with a shake of her head. "Well, he can work alone if he feels like it. *I* say we work together."

Carlos and Felipe agreed. They pushed open the first cabin's door, ready to sweep the daylights out of the place. Except there wasn't enough daylight left to see with. "Where's the light switch?" demanded Carlos, feeling along the rough walls and getting a sliver in his finger. Wasn't *anything* going to go right today?

He finally figured out that the ceiling bulb had a chain hanging from it when Felipe grabbed his arm. "Don't turn it on yet," he hissed. "Look out the window!"

The sun had set, leaving gray twilight behind. In the shadowed woods, Carlos caught a glimpse of something moving. Or someone. Whoever it was didn't want to be seen. The stranger wore a billed cap and a frayed jeans jacket and jeans. It was too dark to see his face, except that Carlos noticed scraggly black hair that hung to his shoulders, thick eyebrows and a close-cropped beard. The man loped from tree to tree with long pauses between each move.

The three kids hunched down beside the screen-covered window. They forgot all about sweeping.

"You suppose this camp gonna have a prowler tonight?" whispered Mashell in a worried voice. Neither boy answered her. Not a pleasant thought.

But then Carlos saw another movement, from between the second and third cabin. "Someone's going out there to meet him. Who do you suppose ... it's *Bronce!*"

They watched in amazement as Mashell's classmate edged toward the woods. Toward the bearded man.

"Is he *crazy* or something?" breathed Felipe. *"Loco?"*

Bronce halted and stared toward their cabin. "We gotta get workin' so he don't realize we watchin' 'im," Mashell whispered. She stood, yanked on the light and began to sweep hard and fast. Felipe joined her. Carlos stayed near the window. Mashell's idea worked. Bronce went back to walking toward the woods.

The man suddenly reached from behind a tree, hooked Bronce's arm and pulled the boy deeper into the woods. Carlos made frantic signals to the others. "That guy's grabbed Bronce! I think he's making off with him!"

"No!" hissed Mashell. She dropped her broom and scuttled to the window. "But I don't hear nothin'. Wouldn't he be hollerin' or puttin' up a fight?"

Felipe hunched down beside them. "The way he was going—like, sneaky, you know? I think he's meeting that guy about something."

"I'm gonna find out." Carlos hurried to the door with the others at his heels. They tiptoed outside and skulked toward the back side of the cabin with their backs pressed against the bark-covered logs. The twilight had darkened to night. The air felt cold and crickets and frogs filled it with trills and breeps. No sounds of a struggle. No shouts for help.

Carlos heard soft voices though, nearby. He dropped to his hands and knees and crawled toward the woods, ordering the others to stay near the cabin with sharp waves of his hands. He reached a pine tree. Then a boulder half as large as a car. He had to move slowly and with nerve-wrenching carefulness. He mustn't make a *sound*.

He crept around the boulder, wincing as a dried leaf crackled under his feet. Maybe they'd think he was a squirrel looking for a late-night snack. The voices kept on, anyway. And now, at last, he could hear words.

"It's unfortunate that you drew attention to yourself," the man said in cross between a murmur and a whisper.

"But they didn't discover anything!" answered Bronce. He spoke softly too, and sounded eager to please and scared, like a whipped dog cowering before his master.

"No harm done, I guess. Now, here's where I want you to leave it. You've seen the creek that runs into Pine Lake, right?"

"Yeah."

"At its mouth, where the stream widens, you'll see an old pine stump. Tomorrow night, leave it inside the big hole at its base. Okay?"

"Okay. An' I'm sorry I messed up."

"Don't worry about it," said the man. "Do you have any questions?"

He had Bronce repeat his instructions. Then he bade the boy goodnight and Carlos heard the rustle of someone hurrying away through the woods. He bit his lip and hunkered down near the rock. Bronce passed by on the other side without seeing him, thank goodness.

Carlos waited several minutes before he carefully rose to his feet. He saw lights in cabins four and five. Felipe and Mashell apparently had sense enough to dash inside so Bronce wouldn't know someone had eavesdropped on him.

He crawled to cabin four and peeked in the window. Bronce was busy sweeping. He pulled away—before the sixth grader saw him—and hurried to number five. Mashell and Felipe were working fast and hard, but they stopped the moment Carlos arrived and talked in excited whispers. They were as curious as he was. What was Bronce going to leave in the tree? And should they tell an adult about the boy's secret meeting?

"Let's not do anything 'til we see what he puts there," suggested Mashell.

The boys agreed. They finished cleaning the cabins to Stan's satisfaction and joined the other children as the campfire meeting began. Bronce didn't say a word to them, and Carlos fought not to stare at him. What *was* he going to leave in the tree?

They'd find out tomorrow night.

* * * * * * * *

The campfire circle didn't last long enough for Carlos. He couldn't decide which he liked better: staring at the fire or singing with forty other kids as Miss Lindstrom strummed her guitar. He enjoyed Mr. Hansen's story too, about the creation of the universe. The boy already knew he was describing the first chapter of the Bible. Or some of it, anyway. Mr. Hansen stopped at the part about God making the moon and stars and let them lean their heads back and stare.

Carlos had never seen the sky looking like this—jet black, clear and cold, with stars like diamond dust. Jagged silhouettes of pine trees, blacker still, made a frame around this section of space that the clearing let them see. The boy felt awestruck and small in comparison to those millions and millions of stars and planets and galaxies.

The group sang "Jesus Loves Me" and he felt even more awed. *Lord, You really made all this stuff and You still care about me? I gotta be as tiny as a grasshopper to You.*

"Yes, Jesus loves me . . . ," the kids sang.

Carlos found himself smiling, and felt as warm inside as the fire's embers, that glowed red like stove burners set on high. The leaders ended the meeting by passing around brownies and hot chocolate. "Can't we roast marshmallows?" asked Mashell. The two boys joined in her begging.

"We'll have lots of other nights around the fire," Miss Lindstrom told them.

Before he wanted to, Carlos was leaning against the cement walls of a long bathroom with several sinks and stalls, waiting his turn to brush his teeth, splash dust and soot off his face and use the toilet.

Bronce stood in line too, sullen and silent as ever. Another sixth grader piped up, "Hey, Bronce, you gonna listen to some tunes tonight?"

"Yeah. Crank up that radio, man!" added another.

"Shut up!" barked Bronce in a voice that made Carlos shudder. More boys would have joined in the teasing if Stan, who was waiting outside the door, hadn't stepped in and cut them off.

Bronce looked like he wanted to kill the whole crowd. Felipe gave Carlos a worried glance. He knew what his best friend was thinking. *Do we really wanna snoop in on this guy's business? If he catches us, we're dead!*

But he knew they'd be too curious to let the mystery rest. They quickly cleaned up and trotted to their tent.

The night had gone from chilly to downright cold. Carlos had griped at the space his heavy jacket took up in his suitcase, but now he was glad Mama made him pack it. And he hoped two blankets would be enough.

Felipe had a sleeping bag. He had a flashlight too, that made the green nylon walls glow like a leaf held up in sunlight. Too bad it didn't give off any warmth! Carlos zipped the tent shut and took off his shoes. "I'm sleeping in my clothes tonight! " he muttered. "I'll freeze in my PJs!"

Felipe was already snuggled in his sleeping bag and he hadn't bothered changing into pajamas, either. Carlos spread his blankets one on top of the other. Then he stretched himself out near their edges and grasped them as he rolled over and over, wrapping them around him like a tube. Mama had taught him to do this when an earthquake forced his family to sleep outside for a whole week. Now all he had to do was flop the end under his feet and he had a sort of sleeping bag.

Foam pads came with the tent, just large enough for one sleeper each. They were three inches thick and felt firm to the touch. But when he lay on his, Carlos still felt the ground as hard as concrete. When he flopped on his side his hipbones felt like knife blades. On his back, rocks dug into his shoulders. And was there a tree root underneath him?

He couldn't toss and turn too much or he'd unwrap himself, and the cold air seemed to delight in sweeping in and chilling whatever he didn't have covered.

Brr! This could be a long night.

Felipe turned off his flashlight and the two boys whispered about the camp and the trip and about what they'd find in Bronce's tree stump tomorrow night. But soon Felipe's side of the conversation stopped. His breathing became slow and steady. Murmurs and giggles from other tents faded away, leaving the crickets and frogs, which only sang louder as the night went on.

Carlos felt tired too, but cold air kept seeping into his makeshift sleeping bag. *Maybe I'll put my jacket on,* he decided. He sat up as quietly as he could and felt for his suitcase. It wasn't hard to find in the dark, nor was his jacket. But as he pulled his coat free, something came with it and plopped to the floor. His hands groped to find it and came upon smooth, cold plastic. No, paper. This thing was a puffy bag. It had lots of things inside it that rustled when he shook it.

What in the world? Oh! Of course! His mind shot
back to lunchtime at the highway rest stop. Mama had
packed too much food for him. He'd shoved this packet in
his suitcase so he wouldn't have to carry so many things.
He'd forgotten all about it by the time the other campers
were placing their snacks in bear-proof food lockers.

But here it was, in his tent, in his hands, and *not* locked
away. An unopened bag of potato chips. His heart raced.
Mr. Hansen told them a thing like this could draw a bear!
What should he *do* with it? Find an adult? They'd all be
asleep by now. Lock it away himself? *How?* He didn't
have keys to the boxes! Maybe he should just toss it in the
woods. That way, the bear could have a midnight snack
without coming into camp.

But the thought of wandering around in dark wilderness
by himself made him feel sick and shaky. What if he met
the bear out *there?* What if he got lost? He didn't even like
the idea of unzipping the tent.

Felipe started to snore, which made Carlos feel lonely,
as well as scared and cold. He was the only one in the
world awake. Would he get any sleep at all? He decided to
stay put and hope for the best. *The bag's not even open,* he

tried to assure himself. *I bet a bear can't smell anything from it.*

The boy wrapped it in a wad of clothes and stuffed it down in his suitcase, just to make sure. Then he tied the case shut as tightly as he could. The boy cocooned himself in his blankets again and made himself lie still. His jacket made him feel much warmer. Drowsiness began to cloak him.

Until something he heard made him wide awake. Leafy rustles that sounded like the footsteps the bearded man made in the woods. He sat up, pawed for Felipe's flashlight, and clicked it on.

The beam hit his friend in the eyes. Felipe flinched, moaned and blinked. It took him several seconds to fully wake up. Then he sat up, looking disgusted.

"What's your problem, waking me up!" he demanded. Carlos was too frightened to answer him. The footsteps were getting closer, and mixed with them, low and deep like a dog with a bass voice, he heard grunts: *ruh-ruh. Ruh-ruh.*

The tent began to shake. Something struck the rear wall. Carlos thought he saw a giant fist outlined in the tent fabric. Then the nylon ripped open and he stared at a huge black paw with curved claws.

Cold, smooth cloth and darkness engulfed him. The tent had collapsed! Carlos punched and kicked the fabric away, only to have it flop back around him. And he yelled as he never had before. *"Help! A bear! A BEAR! He's gonna eat us!"*

He could feel Felipe struggling too, and heard him give strangled, wordless screams. Had the bear *gotten* him? And muffled by the fabric draped around his ears, he picked up gasps and cries of shock and running feet as his fellow campers woke up and noticed their intruder.

He wrapped his arms around his head. Surely, any second, the bear would pounce on him. Bite him. Bat him around with those massive paws. Maybe even pick him up in its teeth and carry him away. And he couldn't do a thing about it. He was *trapped.*

A loud voice carried across the camp and cut through his panic. *"Boys!* Unzip the tent and get out," ordered Mr. Hansen. *"Don't run* or the bear may chase you. Just stand still until I tell you what else to do."

The zipper! He'd forgotten all about it. Carlos scrambled to find it and opened it with a sharp *hhzz*. He crawled outside with his eyes squinched shut, certain he was about to feel fangs clamping on him. But nothing happened. He rose to his feet with his eyes still closed.

The boy lifted one eyelid enough to see a thick-furred black bear standing on all fours, a tent-length away. It must have been the mix of moonlight and shadows that made its chest look as wide as a door and its head as large as a lion's.

It was staring at him.

His eyes shot wide open. Behind him, he heard Felipe struggle out of the tent. His friend stood, whimpering softly, but Carlos was too scared to turn and look at him. He was too scared to move at all.

"Okay!" yelled Mr. Hansen. "Come *slowly* toward my light."

What light? Mr. Hansen was probably standing beside his cabin, near the woods behind them. Which meant the boy had to turn his head to see his flashlight beam. But he didn't want to take his eyes off the bear for a second. Not for a *millisecond*. Because that's when it would attack. He just knew it.

"You've got to start moving," Mr. Hansen ordered them. "Slow and easy. Come on, you can do it."

Glancing over his shoulder at the light was the hardest thing Carlos had ever done. But he knew where the camp director was, now. He began to walk backwards, dragging Felipe with him. *Lord Jesus, keep the bear off us, please! Don't let him eat us!*

The bear began to claw the tent.

Step by step, foot by foot, yard by yard, they put distance between them and the giant animal, who never looked up from its work of tearing the pup tent to pieces. Carlos' muscles felt like twisted ropes about to snap and he kept his eyes glued to the creature.

He should have been watching where he was going. His foot hit a tight, angled cord—someone's tent support—and he toppled over with a yelp, pulling Felipe and the tent down with him. His friend was back on his feet in a blink, hollering with terror and running for everything he was worth. Carlos followed at his heels, screaming too.

They would have raced headlong into the woods if Mr. Hansen hadn't blocked them. "Okay, *okay,* you can stop now, boys! You're safe."

Carlos' muscles untwisted in a burst of relief. *Thank You, Jesus! Thank You, Jesus!* Mr. Hansen placed a strong hand on his shoulder and it seemed as though warmth passed from it to every part of his body.

All twenty of the boys and many of the girls stood clustered on Mr. Hansen's porch, staring in wide-eyed silence at the dark form in the midst of the clearing. They could hear it bashing and scraping and biting whatever held the food. Carlos knew. His suitcase.

It huffed and grunted, too. Until a harsh, yellow-white spotlight hit the bear. It looked up and gave a startled snort. But before it could run, a gunshot blasted and echoed from the pines. The animal jerked as though stung by a hundred hornets at once, then galloped away with whining groans. Carlos heard the crackles of something heavy falling in thick under-growth. Then silence, even from the crickets and frogs.

"Somebody *killed* it!" Carlos cried, high-pitched. "What for? It didn't hurt us!"

"The bear's not dead," Mr. Hansen explained. "A park ranger shot it with a tranquilizing dart. It'll be transported a hundred miles from here, and hopefully it won't ransack any other tents."

He shook his head. "Once a bear discovers campgrounds are an easy source of food, even painful darts won't stop it. If this one keeps raiding tents, it'll be killed."

He started walking and Carlos and Felipe followed him. They reached the ripped-up tent and Mr. Hansen guided his flashlight over the shredded nylon and scattered clothing and broken pieces of suitcase. "What drew that bear to you?"

Felipe shrugged. Carlos said nothing and prayed the man wouldn't find the reason. But Mr. Hansen suddenly bent down and snatched something from under Carlos' pajamas. He didn't need to look at the man's face to know he was furious. He held the thing in the light for the boys to see.

A mangled bag of potato chips.

* * * * * * * *

Morning sunlight gleamed off the varnished cedar-log walls in Mr. Hansen's office. Carlos sat on a folding chair, staring at his lap. The camp was completely quiet, except for the chitterings and whistles of arguing birds that floated in through the screened window. He was the only kid left around.

The others, including Felipe, were off on a nature hike. Carlos wished with all his heart he was with them. But he confessed that the chips were his. He alone had known they were in the tent. So he alone was in big trouble.

"I found the bag in my suitcase when it was way late. Like, midnight or something," he mumbled. "I couldn't figure out a way to get it into the food lockers. And it was just a *little* bag of chips."

Mr. Hansen sat at his desk with his arms folded across his chest, looking angry. "That *little* bag of chips may have cost that bear his life. And he could have killed *you*."

Carlos grimaced. "Are you gonna send me home early?" He'd rather die. He'd rather get sent to Siberia.

The director sat in silence for what seemed an hour. "You feel awful about this, don't you?" he finally said.

Regret welled up and Carlos blurted out, "That bear, it was so—*grand*. I can't stand the thought of it getting killed because of me. I didn't know what to do with the chips, you know? I figured all you grownups were asleep. I tell you, I didn't sneak it in the tent for a snack or anything. After lunch, I just shoved it in my suitcase and forgot about it." He punched his thigh with his fist. *"Man,* for stupid!"

Mr. Hansen unfolded his arms. "What should you have done when you found it?"

"Turned it over to somebody. But wouldn't you have been pretty ticked off if I'd got you out of bed at midnight just to give you a bag of chips?"

A smile sneaked onto the corners of Mr. Hansen's lips. "Maybe. But I wouldn't have let you know it. I would have thanked you for being responsible and grumbled to my wife about it after you left." He raised one eyebrow. "The way it turned out, I lost a lot more sleep, don't you think?"

"You gonna send me home early?" Carlos asked again, fighting the urge to plead with Mr. Hansen. *Please let me stay! Please? I really like it here. I'll be good, really! . . .*

The director cleared his throat. "I can't promise that the bear will stop raiding campgrounds. You know what will happen to him if he keeps it up."

"He'll be shot with real bullets." The boy closed his eyes and the image tore at his heart like a predator's claws. The bear was too magnificent to die that way.

"I think that's punishment enough for you. So, you can stay."

Relief washed over Carlos. He didn't have to go home in disgrace to an empty neighborhood! He didn't have to listen to the others talk while only imagining the fun they had. "Are you gonna let Felipe and me sleep in a cabin again?"

Mr. Hansen broke into a grin. "No, sir! Those are reserved for adult guests, not kids who are here to learn to camp. You'll be back in a tent with the others tonight. Speaking of the others, they'll be returning from the hike in a few minutes. Why don't you wait for them at the boat dock?"

"Can I go canoeing this afternoon?"

"You're cleared to join whatever activity you want."

Carlos let out a whoop. *Thanks,* Mr. Hansen!" He bolted for the door, but stopped short. "Will I ever know if that bear lives or dies?"

Mr. Hansen had begun sorting a stack of mail. He paused

with a letter in his hand, then used it to thoughtfully scratch the side of his face. "Actually, yes. Yosemite National Park's wildlife techicians put a radio collar on him so they could monitor his movements." He tapped his cheek with the letter. "Maybe you'd like to see the equipment they use."

"Yeah!"

"I'll see what I can do. And I'll ask them to let us know what the bear does and what they have to do with him. They'll know if he raids another camp. Let's hope he doesn't."

"I'm gonna *pray* he doesn't," Carlos vowed.

5

Mashell felt delighted that Carlos was able to stay. It
was bad enough that he'd been attacked by a bear. Getting
sent home early would have made his week (and everyone
else's) the worst. She and Anna, Felipe and several other
Good News Club kids met at the boat dock after lunch,
dressed in swimsuits and life vests with camp towels
around their necks. Bronce and three other sixth-grade
boys chose to canoe, too. The afternoon was calm and the
sunshine felt hot.

"You wanna tell me why it's warm enough for swimmin'
durin' the day and freezin' at night?" Mashell asked, not really
expecting an answer from her friends.

"Because we're in the mountains," said a female voice
behind them. Becky Lindstrom and Stan walked onto the
dock, making its flat boards jiggle under everyone's feet.

She went on, "At higher elevations, the air is thinner. You feel the heat of the sun more. And at night, everything cools off more quickly. It's also like moving to a different climate—Minnesota, or some other northern state."

"Now for a lesson on how to handle a canoe," said Stan in a businesslike voice. "First of all, it's most important that you wear your life vest *at all times*. It could save you from drowning. Let's practice putting it on and securing it."

The kids stared at him, confused. They were already wearing them. Miss Lindstrom whispered this to Stan, who cleared his throat and proceeded to check their fasteners for tightness. "Just see that you don't take them off," he added gruffly.

"As for maneuvering the canoe, it isn't as easy as it looks. Canoes are tippy, as you'll find out. The first trick is getting aboard. Becky and I will demonstrate."

The two adults pushed a slim, silver-colored watercraft into the lake and guided it to the end of the dock. Miss Lindstrom gingerly stepped into it. The canoe shimmied back and forth dangerously and she grabbed Stan's shirt with a gasp, nearly ripping it off him. Mashell had to clap her hand over her mouth to keep from laughing.

But the young lady managed to sit safely. "As you can see," said Stan, straightening his messed-up T-shirt and lowering his leg into the canoe, "it's very important that you step *exactly* in the middle. Got that? In the *mid* . . . ."

He never finished his sentence because he made the mistake of looking at his pupils instead of where he needed to step. His foot landed off-center and pushed the canoe away. Stan wound up spread-eagled with one foot still on the dock. But only for a moment. His foot slipped and he twisted in midair, making a frantic grab for the dock. He missed, of course, and made a face-first *splat* in the water.

His splash was followed in the next instant by another, almost as magnificent, from Miss Lindstrom. He also capsized the canoe.

Mashell laughed so hard she had to sit as the two adults dragged themselves and the canoe out of the water. "How not to do it," said Stan flatly.

It took awhile for the kids to catch their breath and wipe their eyes. And still, giggles kept breaking out. Even from Bronce. He seemed much more himself today.

They discovered for themselves that keeping a canoe upright and moving wasn't so easy. It was a good thing they wore swimsuits! Anna and Mashell managed to get safely into their canoe. But Carlos and Felipe's tipped over and instead of righting it and climbing back in, they swam toward the girls'.

"Oh, no you don't!" shouted Mashell, grabbing a paddle and beating the water white in a frenzied attempt to *move.* She quickly realized that one person paddling on one side only pushed the canoe in circles.

"Anna! Other side, *quick!"* She handed the other paddle to her friend and both girls slapped the water to a froth. But they weren't making much headway.

"Work together!" yelled Becky from the dock. *"Time* your strokes. Cut them deep into the water and create a *rhythm!"*

But her instruction came too late. The girls had their paddles poised for the first mighty stoke when two pairs of hands popped out of the water, grasped the same side of the canoe, and *pulled.*

Mashell went over with a shriek. Oo*hoo,* the water was cold! The shock made her wonder if she'd ever breathe again. She heard laughter, muffled by the water lapping around her ears, and saw two pairs of scrawny legs dangling

beside the upside-down canoe. She raised her face. *Okay.*
Anna was fine, treading water and giggling. The boys
caught sight of Mashell's dripping head and pointed and
jeered and hooted.

Blast this life preserver! If she could swim underwater,
they'd get the dunking of their lives! She pursed her lips
and fumbled with the buckles. *How 'bout I just wear this
thing in the canoe?* she thought.

Stan was watching her. *"Mashell!* Don't even think
about it!" he bellowed.

"But I'm a good swimmer!" Her protests did no good.
She made the best of it by catching a paddle as it floated by
and using it to send tidal waves of water into the boys' faces.
They couldn't get away very quickly because they were
hindered by vests, too. And they made a feeble attempt to
splash her back, but slapping hands were no match for a
fiberglass canoe paddle. She felt vindicated, anyway.

The two girls decided to swim a little before getting
back in the canoe. Mashell was used to the lake's
temperature by now. The water was so *clear!* She kicked
along face-down, staring at the muddy bottom some ten feet
away, strewn with pebbles and boulders and sunken logs

covered with fuzz. *Cool!* She even saw a crayfish
squirming through a patch of waving seaweed.

The two girls turned the canoe over, pushed it back to
shore, stepped in and tried to paddle the way Miss
Lindstrom told them, with deep strokes and at the same
time, in rhythm. It worked. So well, in fact, that they
wound up beating everybody at races (to Carlos and
Felipe's chagrin). They were even faster than Bronce and
another sixth-grade boy—the biggest guys in camp!

Bronce congratulated them with a good-natured grin.

The Good News Kids were all in favor of setting up an
official race. But the afternoon was waning and recreation
time would be over by the time they arranged it. "Maybe
another day," said Stan.

Mashell wasn't too disappointed. Her arms, especially
the upper muscles that attached to her chest, were throbbing. *"Girlfriend,* are we gonna be sore tomorrow!" she
moaned to Anna.

Her friend smiled ruefully. "It was worth it, though."

The camp had showers in the same style of buildings as
the bathrooms—cold concrete floors, gray cement walls,
fluorescent lights. Each stall had whitewashed walls and a

yellow, plastic curtain hanging in front. Not the coziest place to clean up in. But it was better than being dirty.

She and Anna sat on a log and braided each other's soaking-wet hair, to the great interest of the other girls (who were all younger). Anna put a tight braid in Mashell's coarse, shoulder-length hair, then twisted it into a knot and put a hair wrap around it. Just the way Mashell liked it— neat, out-of-the-way, hassle-free.

Mashell ran a comb through Anna's wavy black hair. "Girl, you know how *long* this is gettin'? Almost halfway down your back!"

Anna nodded. "I've never had it cut. Just the ends trimmed, you know?"

Mashell gave her friend a French braid and it turned out well, if she said so herself. Several girls begged Mashell to give them the same hairstyle. "What am I, the camp hair- dresser?" she grumbled. She wouldn't admit she enjoyed basking in the admiration of the younger kids. She gave three of them French braids. Anna did three more.

"Your braids wind up so smooth and even," Anna remarked. "I wish I could get my hair to look that good."

"Ooh, girl, you think I can do a French braid on *myself?*
I wind up jumpin' 'round the bathroom with my hands
in my hair, *screamin'*." She laughed loudly and Anna
joined in. The other girls were too busy admiring each
other's hairstyles.

They needed jackets and long pants by supper time.
Spaghetti and meatballs, one of Mashell's favorites. (After
all the canoe racing, she was *starving*.) She was fascinated,
watching the adults cook it in pots set on grates over three
large fires. "Look at that water go *crazy!*" she told Anna.
"It never boils that hard on the stove at home!"

Stan overheard them. "There are two reasons for that.
One, this is a really hot fire. If it weren't for intense heat,
the spaghetti noodles would take forever to cook. Two,
we're at a higher elevation, which means the air is thinner
and there's less pressure from the atmosphere. Water boils
at a lower temperature."

She was glad to hear they weren't going to be delayed.
She turned her gaze to the meatballs, frying in pans (oh, the
aroma!), going from raw to sizzling brown in minutes. The
cooks dropped them into the red sauce, heated it to bubbling

and let the kids line up. It was all Mashell could do to keep from pushing to the front.

They had lettuce salad too, and milk to drink and chocolate pudding for dessert. Food didn't taste this good at home, either. Not even a pine-needle-and-dirt-coated meatball that someone accidentally dropped could squelch her appetite.

Carlos and Felipe sat across from her and Anna. Carlos caught her eye and nodded over his shoulder. Bronce sat at the table behind them, among a cluster of sixth-grade boys, talking and joking. But as the meal ended, the brooding nervousness he'd shown before came back. He began tapping his fingers and glancing toward the woods. Toward Pine Lake Creek.

The sun sank behind the mountains and early evening twilight settled in. All the young campers helped wash dishes and tidy the eating area. Mashell and Carlos and Felipe did garbage duty, sticking close together as they picked up napkins and plastic forks and paper cups. They never took their eyes off Bronce.

They decided to let Anna in on what was going on. Mashell beckoned her to the garbage cans and whispered in her ear while she tied knots in the plastic bags.

"Shouldn't we tell somebody like Stan or Miss Lindstrom?" Anna asked, full of concern.

"Yeah, but we gotta know *what* to tell 'em! What's he leavin' in the tree?"

Anna looked worried. "What if that guy comes while we're looking?"

"We'll keep a eye out for him!" Mashell busied herself tugging open the garbage can's spring-loaded, bear-proof lid and stuffing the bag into it. Anna became too distracted helping her to ask any more questions, which was exactly what Mashell wanted.

Free time was about to start. The four kids gathered at a table to watch Bronce finish wiping dishes. "Don't be starin' at 'im!" hissed Mashell. "Just glance once in awhile. An' even then, don't look right at 'im!"

Carlos looked disgusted. "Why don't you tell us something we don't know?"

"Bet he leaves now," she said.

"I hope we get back in time for the campfire," added Felipe.

Anna pursed her lips. "I hope we get back at all!"

"We'll be *fine,* girlfriend!" Mashell suddenly stiffened. "Hold on! He leavin'!" They saw him disappear in his pup tent, then come out again wearing a bulky jacket. Carlos spoke in an excited whisper. "Look how he's got his arms around his stomach, like he's cold or something. Don't believe it! I say he's holding something inside his coat!"

Mashell was first to stand up, stretch, and say in a loud voice, "Let's go take a walk." The others imitated her actions, trying to look casual.

They stayed as far behind him as they could without losing sight of him. Which wasn't easy, since they didn't want him to see *them*. Mashell hoped they'd look like just four more kids milling around the campground.

Bronce never gave up glancing over his shoulders. "Why he have to be so alert!" griped Mashell. "He gonna make it really hard when we get past the campground."

Felipe said eagerly, "We'll make like guerrilla soldiers, you know? Get down and crawl."

Anna made a face that expressed how Mashell felt too. *Gross! What if there's bugs and snakes? What if I get my clothes all ripped up?* But she wasn't going to say anything and she knew Anna wouldn't either. They weren't about to pull a *girl thing*.

They reached the woods. Bronce was already well inside; they could hear him pushing his way through the bushes, snapping sticks under his feet. *He goin' about as quiet as a hippo!* thought Mashell.

All the better for them. The more noise he made the less chance he'd hear them. "Here's what we do," Carlos whispered. "We can't keep moving steady or he'll hear us. We gotta each pick our own trees and whatever to hide behind. Go from one to the other and then wait, you know?"

They understood. Anna looked frightened. "It's so *dark* in there, though! We'll never find our way back!" She was right. The woods' deep shadows made it look as though night had already fallen within it.

"Yes, we will!" Felipe pulled a long, slender cylinder out of his pocket. His flashlight!

Mashell grinned. "Glad you got *that!*" She didn't admit it, but she, too, was afraid of getting lost in the woods at night.

Bronce's noises were fading. "Let's go!" Carlos ordered them. He bent forward, hunched his shoulders like an Indian on a game hunt and tiptoed into the woods. The others followed, trying to move as quietly.

It was slow work, skulking from pine trunk to boulder to stump. Mashell could hardly see anything. Her legs brushed against ferns and bushes. The ground seemed mostly bare, without much grass. She tripped over a tree root and her hands and knees thumped down on a thick, springy cushion of dried pine needles. She hopped silently to her feet and made it to the next trunk.

Was Bronce still walking? She couldn't hear anything but the gentle rustle of Anna's feet as she scooted to a tree nearby. The boys stood frozen against a boulder as large as a house and Carlos was motioning for everybody to stop. Mashell had time to notice something sticky on her hands. Pine sap! Its smell made her think of Christmas trees.

The crickets and frogs began their evening concert. And her ears caught a distant sound, a sort of whisper. Was a breeze starting?

Carlos led them to another boulder, large enough for all four of them to stand behind. Mashell felt clumps of soft moss and brittle lichen under her fingers. And now she knew what she was hearing. The creek! It made a merry sound—a constant chitter mixed with high and low ploops and plops and bubbles.

But she wasn't paying much attention. Her eyes were riveted to a wide stump that had once been the trunk of an enormous redwood pine. It still stood about ten feet tall and its top was twisted and jagged. The tree itself lay stretched out many feet away with dead branch stubs circling it.

The stump was in a small clearing that led to the lake, and the light around it was bright compared to the shadowy woods. She could easily see Bronce shoving something into a black-edged, tepee-shaped hole that a fire had burned in the stump's base. She bit her lip and waited for him to finish. Would he walk past their rock? Would he see them? If he did, what excuse could they possibly make for being here? *Oh hi, Bronce! Guess you decided to take a nature hike, too!*

He straightened up, looked around and walked toward them! Mashell pointed to the side of the boulder opposite where he'd pass. She could have saved herself the trouble. Carlos, Felipe, and Anna were already scrambling for it.

Quietly, you guys! But to her horror, it was one of *her* feet that found a branch and cracked it. She dropped down to a baseball-catcher kneel. Bronce stopped walking and she knew that he was staring. But she couldn't risk a look or he'd see *her.*

"Mister? That you?" the sixth-grader whispered hoarsely.

Nobody moved. Nobody breathed. Finally, Bronce let out a puff of air. "Just a squirrel," he muttered, and hurried away without another word.

After several long minutes, Carlos straightened up with a sigh of relief. "That was too close!"

Mashell would have agreed with him out loud if she hadn't been so distracted by the throb of feeling rushing back to her calves and feet. But then her eyes fell on the tree stump. She gave the others a bright grin and they raced toward it, too excited to be quiet now. The mystery was about to be solved!

Felipe aimed his flashlight into the pitch black hole and the beam reflected off three packages. Carlos tugged one of them forward enough for them to get a better look. It was a square of clear plastic film—about the size of a fast food hamburger box—wrapped around white stuff. Powdery white stuff.

Mashell felt the warmth drain from her face. She could tell by their expressions that the others knew what this stuff was too.

Cocaine.

"He's a drug smuggler!" breathed Felipe. "How'd he get it here?"

"*Who cares?*" croaked Mashell. Her eyes were growing wet with fear. They were in terrible danger. Carlos looked around wildly. "That guy in the beard's gonna pick it up. We gotta get *outta* here!"

He dropped the package as though it had turned into a blazing ember. As it hit the ground, a furious voice yelled, *"Hernandez! What you doin'? Spyin' on me?"*

Bronce!

They whirled and stared, all four of them too flustered to say anything.

But the worst hadn't happened yet. Mashell heard fast footsteps behind her, then a hand clamped on her shoulder with a grip that made her cry out in pain and fright.

The hand spun her around and she found herself looking into the barrel of a black handgun. It was held by the bearded man.

6

Mashell was so scared she felt nauseated. *Father God, You gotta save us!* she prayed. *Get us away from this guy! I won't ever spy on anybody again!*

Anna started to scream and the man cut her off with a savage shout. "Be *quiet!*" He sounded like he had sand in his throat. "All of you stand perfectly still and *shut up* or I'll shoot the girl."

Mashell trembled and tears streamed down her face. Her voice quavered. "Don't kill me, mister. Please don't kill me. We won't tell nobody."

He glowered at her and she stopped talking (and crying) with a gulp. Then he scowled at Bronce, who looked as frightened as the others. "Couldn't you *tell* you were being followed? They made enough noise for an army! I watched them all the way from the camp!" He shook his head. "Pathetic! But what else can I expect from city brats?"

"I'm-I'm *sorry.* I did just what you said...."

"Uh-huh. I'm surprised all the cops and park rangers for fifty miles haven't gathered here." He glanced around, as though they would pop out of the trees any second. "Well, I'm not dead yet."

He looked at Carlos. "Pick up the packages."

The boy obeyed at once. He thrust his head and shoulders into the hole, grabbed the two inside and tossed them near the first. Then he tried to stand with all three in his arms, but they were slippery. One dropped to the ground.

"Help him!"

Felipe jumped to the command. The man changed his grip from Mashell's shoulder to her upper arm. Then he made her run beside him to a tree and, still holding her (as if she was *about* to fight him), stretched his gun hand toward a large flashlight lying on the ground beside a dusty, olive-green backpack. His jacket sleeve pulled back and she caught sight of the ugliest scratches she'd ever seen. There were two of them, side by side, one about as wide as a magic marker line and the other like a pencil mark. They curved down his arm like snakes. They were both red and swollen and the fatter one had patches of dried blood on it.

She grimaced in disgust, but she had no sympathy for him. He didn't notice. He was too busy trying to hold the gun and pick up the flashlight with the same hand. Finally, he gave an angry grunt and let go of her arm. *"You* pick it up and hold it!"

She meekly obeyed. He snatched up the backpack, zipped it open and ordered Carlos and Felipe to drop the hateful squares of white powder inside. Then he closed it and slung it across his back. He grasped Mashell's arm again and started walking rapidly. "All four of you, come on!"

"What are you gonna *do?"* asked Bronce in a panic-stricken voice. "You ain't gonna *hurt* us . . . ? I *did* my job!"

"Your next job is to *shut up!"*

He led them at a trot. Darkness was draping down, leaving only a rose-orange glow behind black mountains. Which meant they had to hurry through the dark woods with only the flashlight's bobbing circle to guide them. Branches whipped Mashell's face and she constantly tripped on roots and rocks. So did the others.

The path wasn't level, either. It rose and fell, sometimes steeply, until they nearly had to scrabble on hands and knees with thumping hearts and aching lungs, gasping air and groaning from hurting muscles. But the man didn't let up. For hours, it seemed.

* * * * * * * *

Carlos blamed himself for the danger they were in. *I had to get curious about what Bronce was going to hide in the stump, didn't I! Why didn't I mind my own business? We're probably gonna get killed!*

They'd scrambled along for what felt like half the night, through a narrow, rocky valley walled by pine-covered mountains. It had a sluggish stream wandering through it, much slower and quieter than Pine Lake Creek, with dry spots and pools edged with scum.

Bright moonlight shining through tree branches turned the trail into a confusing patchwork of silver light and shadow. Carlos tripped for the hundredth time and fell hard.

Oof! His chest slammed against a large fallen log. The wind was knocked out of him. His lungs felt glued together and all he could do was lie on his back, hold his ribs and gulp tiny bits of air. Would he suffocate? Were his ribs broken? The pain made his eyes water.

He couldn't cry out, either. No one knew he was hurt. The flashlight's beam faded until bushes blocked it from his view. The hustled footsteps grew faint.

Carlos was left alone.

He wanted to scream with fright and run after the others as fast as he could. He'd rather face the bearded man and his gun than get lost in the wilderness! If only he could *move!*

But his lungs wouldn't let him. He'd had the wind knocked out of him before and he knew if he lay still long enough, his breathing would return to normal. But how long would he have to wait? Until the others were gone?

The ache lessened. His lungs relaxed and his throbbing muscles stopped trembling. He drew a deep breath and sat up. Silence such as he had never known wrapped around him. It filled his ears. It went deep inside. It wouldn't give way to the meager noises of the living either, such as the rustling of his feet, but seemed to stifle them.

He cupped his hands to shout. His voice would echo,
wouldn't it? They'd hear it and come back, wouldn't they?
Then he stopped. Did he really *want* them to? He pictured
the bearded man's beat-up cap, stringy hair and thick
eyebrows locked in a frown. And the gun, next to Mashell's
head . . . .

Carlos' heart thumped as he realized what had just
happened. He'd gotten *away!* He wasn't the bearded man's
captive anymore! Now what should he do? Sneak after
them and knock the man out? What if he got caught again?
What if the man shot *him?* And how would he ever find
them in the first place?

He hit his left fist into his right hand several times, like
a pitcher deciding if he should throw a fast ball or a curve.
He *had* to help them somehow, before the bearded man hurt
Mashell or Bronce or Felipe or Anna, his very own *sister!*

He knew what he'd do! He'd find his way back to
camp. All he had to do was walk back in the direction
they'd come, right? Just follow this narrow valley until it
opened up at the woods. But then, how would he ever find
the camp? Maybe he'd find a trail he could follow. Then
he'd get Mr. Hansen to call the police. They'd rescue the
other kids and arrest the bearded man!

He tried to ignore the voice inside him that nagged, *You're lost. You'll never find your way back.* Instead, he prayed. *Lord Jesus, help me please!* He was on his feet the next moment. But before he moved, something up ahead caught his eye. A tiny twinkle bobbing through the undergrowth, coming toward him. A flashlight beam.

The bearded man? Who else would it be? He was looking for him, of course! Panic tore at Carlos and he cast around for a hiding place. Another rock? A big tree? The fallen log! It was so wide that it came almost to his chest, and it was many yards long. He touched the jagged end nearest him. *Please be hollow!*

It was solid. The light was getting closer. Carlos ran to the stump's other end, praying it had a hole burned in it. It *did!* He shot inside and crawled as far he could. The log was rough and splintery under his hands and smelled of ashes and mildew and dirt and old wood. And it was darker than he'd ever imagined darkness could be. He'd heard people talk about not being able to see their hands in front of their faces, but he'd never believed them. Until now.

He didn't like being inside the log at all. He kept imagining little crawly things dropping down his neck and creeping up his legs but he didn't dare stop to brush them away. *Keep going, keep going, keep going!*

The boy kept reaching in front of him. He'd come against a dead end soon, he knew, because the hole didn't go all the way through. And he didn't want to bump into it for fear of making noise.

He heard footsteps and froze. The bearded man must be walking by! Carlos sat as quietly as he could and clamped his hands over his mouth. No, he heard several feet. The man still had the others with him.

The gruff voice broke the silence with a swear word, but the man said nothing else. The steps went on and faded away. Then they came back. Suddenly a sharp *thunk* rattled Carlos' ears and made the log shake. He felt like a flea in a snare drum.

"Not hollow," rasped that awful voice. (Thank goodness the log's hole didn't extend the whole length!) "Where's he *hiding?* Well, he can stay lost then! I can't hang around! The bears'll have to find him!"

"Carlos!" cried Anna as the footsteps hurried away. The terror in her voice made him wince. Maybe he was doing the wrong thing! Maybe he was being a coward! It

was up to him to rescue them, wasn't it? *I'll sneak after them! I'll surprise the guy, somehow. I'll steal his gun!*

He scrambled out of the log, ignoring the ashes and fungus and wood chips that covered him. How did they get so far ahead? The bearded man must be making them run! He barely heard their rustling and the light was only a dot that wavered down the trail. The boy loped after them, moaning softly from stiff muscles and praying he wouldn't fall off a hidden cliff.

If only he could fly! The darkness didn't help at all. Fighting through the woods alongside a girl holding a single flashlight was hard enough, but it was nothing compared to this. Roots and logs that he didn't know existed caught his toes and nearly sent him sprawling. The brush was much thicker here too.

Some of the bushes had thorns that snagged his clothes and ripped long, stinging scratches in his hands and on his face. But he couldn't whimper. He couldn't even stop long enough to rub his wounds. The light kept growing smaller and dimmer. Then it disappeared.

He'd lost them.

Carlos forced himself onward. *They're ahead of me,* he promised himself. *They gotta be. If I keep going, I'll catch them 'cause they have to rest sometime.* He strained his ears to hear *anything.* But not even crickets were singing now. Here was that silence again—that filled his ears.

Until the loudest sound he'd heard in hours echoed through the woods—the deep *hrrumm* of a starting engine. He instinctively ducked behind a stump.

Headlight beams arced through the trees and Carlos saw colors—green leaves, rust bark—for the first time since the sun went down. He squinted and stared past the lights. Did the valley open up ahead?

The vehicle's motor sounded deep and angry. An old truck, maybe.

And a driver that was in a hurry. The boy heard a man's voice shouting. No question whose it was. He heard a door squeak open. More commands. A high, young voice protesting. The door slamming shut.

Carlos jumped up and ran. They were *leaving!* He had to go with them—but then he'd get *caught* by the bearded man! What should he do? Indecision stopped him in his tracks.

The thought of spending the night by himself made him feel sick. And how would he ever find his friends and his sister once the man drove away with them? Better to join them again. He could sneak away *later.*

But he'd spent too long deciding. The man pulled the driver's door shut and revved the engine. Carlos heard the roar drop in pitch and slow down as the man shifted into reverse. Then it grumbled higher and louder and faster as the vehicle jounced backwards. The headlight beams rocked and rotated, pulling away and leaving pitch blackness behind them. The truck squawked and rattled, complaining at having to move over rough, roadless ground.

Carlos tore after them, yelling and waving his arms. But it did no good. By the time he reached the clearing the truck was a pair of red taillights and a distant rumble that quickly faded away.

He was left in the dark alpine meadow, lost in the wilderness and alone.

7

Mashell sat with her forehead resting on her drawn-up knees, trying to ignore the bumping and swaying as the old pickup bounced along on—who knew what kind of a road this was? Maybe it wasn't a road at all.

Anna had given herself over to a hard cry, pouring out a whispered prayer between sobs. "Oh, Lord Jesus, help us! And wrap Your arms around Carlos, *please!* Let him—find the camp again! Keep him safe from—from *bears* ...."

Mashell would have joined her if she had any tears left. She'd used them all up on that desperate, horrible run through the wilderness with that man's hand squeezing her upper arm and that gun pointing at her head.

He never let them stop until he realized Carlos was missing. And then, after threatening to shoot them all if the boy didn't appear or if they didn't tell him where he was

hiding, he led them away again. Even faster. Until
Mashell was beyond exhausted. Until numbness clouded
over her pain and fear and worry. She didn't care what
happened anymore.

When the man dragged her and the others to this gross
old pickup and ordered them to crawl in the back, she did so
without a word. The truck box was covered by a battered
camper top. It held nothing but a spare tire—and three kids,
now. Bronce tried to protest. Let him. She didn't care.

Only Anna's misery could break through the cloud. She
raised her head from her knees, forced her eyes open (they
felt like she'd used cement for mascara), and patted Anna's
back. Her words came out slurred. "Carlos'll make it.
He'll be all right."

"What about us?" muttered Bronce. "We're in worse
shape than *he* is!"

Anger briefly burned her fatigue away. "Oh, *really!*
Maybe you'd like to jump outta the truck and join 'im in
the woods!"

"Yeah I would, as a matter of fact! Anything to get
away from this guy."

The only noise for several moments, besides the
creaking, booming truck, was Anna's sniffling.

"What were you *doin'*, gettin' messed up with him,
anyway?" Mashell demanded. Bronce didn't answer.

"He pay you a lot?" piped up Felipe.

Bronce gave him a sideways glance. "Why you wanna
know? So you can be a drug smuggler too? I'm tellin' you,
man! It ain't worth it!"

"Felipe, no!" Anna blurted out

Felipe waved his hands. *"I* don't wanna be a smuggler!
I'm just curious!"

Mashell was too. She hoped the sixth-grade boy
would answer.

"Two hundred dollars."

Her mouth popped open. Felipe whistled. Anna, red-
faced and swollen-eyed, burst into a furious lecture about
the dangers of cocaine to the body and the danger they were
in because of it.

"Relax, girlfriend," said Mashell when she could get a
word in. "I *hate* cocaine! I hate the crack they make outta
it! You should see what it do to my mom. She get like a
zombie. She ain't worth nothin' to nobody when she

smokin' it." She glared at Bronce and her voice turned shrill. "You right! No amount of money's worth *this!* What this guy gonna do to us? Huh?"

Bronce took a sudden interest in his fingers. "I dunno. I just know I'm really scared, man. I never been so scared in my life." His eyes filled up and nearly spilled over. "I wish I'd never got messed up with this drug thing."

He blinked hard and set his jaw and kept himself from crying. But Anna didn't. "And what about *Carlos?*" she wailed.

* * * * * * * *

Carlos sat with his back against an oak tree and tried to calm himself. Hearing his own voice comforted him, somehow. Anything to keep the silence at bay. "Okay, okay. You're gonna be *fine.* Just walk back to camp, you know? You can do it. And don't be scared of the dark. There's nothing out here!"

Except bears and drug dealers.

He wished Peppy were here. No bear would dare attack if he was around! He could almost feel his golden retriever nosing his hand, begging for a back scratch. He longed to bury his chilly hands in Peppy's curly fur. But his jacket's thin pockets would have to do.

The boy shivered from cold and the fear he was trying so hard to fight away. And he was hungry and thirsty and tired. Why couldn't he be lying in a tent all wrapped in blankets right now?

And what was going to happen to his friends and his sister? What if he never saw them again? What if he never saw *anybody* again?

"Lord Jesus, help me get back. Help me be—okay—" Warm tears ran down his cheeks and he hurriedly wiped them away with the back of his sleeve. What did it matter if he cried, anyway? Nobody would know. Nobody was here to see him.

Nobody? "Except You, God." The boy brushed the wetness off his nose with his hand, then dried his fingers on his jeans. Knowing Jesus was right here listening made him feel better. He imagined the Lord sitting with *His* back against the oak. "When You were a kid, did You ever get

lost? If You did, I bet You weren't scared. How could You
be? You *made* this place!"

The stars looked more vivid tonight than he'd ever seen
them. The sky was *thick* with them like spilled sugar on a
black mat. He pursed his lips. "If You could make all those
stars and planets and stuff, You can get me back to camp.
And You can keep Anna and Felipe and Mashell safe, too."
His eyes grew hot as they filled again. "You will, won't You?"

He shook the tears away impatiently. Was he forgetting
something? "Oh yeah. Bronce. Keep him safe." Anger
suddenly welled up, warming him all over. "What did he
smuggle drugs for? Because of him, my sister and my
friends could get *killed!* I don't care *how* much they paid
him! I hope he and that guy go to jail!"

Carlos' hands formed fists in his pocket and his arm
muscles tightened. "I gotta get back to camp! I gotta get
the police after them!" He stood, put his back to the
meadow and began marching—and after three steps tripped
on a tree root.

"Why couldn't I get a flashlight?" he yelled through
gritted teeth. "I *told* Mama I needed one! But *no!* We had
to get diapers for Rosa!"

A deeper fear was setting in. What if he walked headlong into a *bear?* Or, much worse, what if a bear hunted *him?* The boy pictured the huge, rough-furred beast that had mangled his tent twenty-four hours ago, and his eyes watered for a different reason. *Lord, I gotta do this! I gotta get back! Keep the bears away, okay?*

He felt ahead with his hands and walked carefully, sometimes tapping the ground with his toes before stepping, and straining to hear the sound he dreaded most—heavy paws shuffling through undergrowth. But all he heard was the rustle of his own feet.

Finding his way through the valley was easy. It was what he'd do once he left it that worried him. How would he *ever* find Pine Lake Camp? He stared overhead. Maybe he could use the stars to navigate . . . . He'd read about sailors doing that. But the only constellation he knew was the Big Dipper. Polaris, the North Star, was supposed to point north. But he had no idea which of the brighter stars it was. And who knew if the camp was north or west or *whatever* from here?

"There's gotta be a landmark I can go by. Maybe the mountains!" They looked like giant, sleeping dinosaurs,

black against the charcoal sky. One had two humps on top.
Another seemed to have a bald spot. But he hadn't paid
attention to them before, so how was he to know which one
pointed the way to camp?

Carlos stubbed his toes against a rock and decided to
quit staring around. "What else is there?" Talking out loud
definitely made him feel braver. "Lord, will You help me
remember?"

"Let's see. There's the log I hid in. But that's here in this
valley and I know where I'm going at the *moment.*"

He wanted to kick himself. *"Why* didn't I notice
anything else?" He was growing hungrier by the minute
and his thoughts turned to hamburgers and pizza and
spaghetti with meatballs. "I could drink a whole pitcher of
pop, too!"

A glass of water would have been *wonderful.* "Is it safe
to drink from the stream?" He pictured its stagnant pools
and made a face. "Pine Lake Creek would be okay, though.
It's running over rocks and everything. It's still fresh."

Wait a minute! Pine Lake Creek led right back to camp!
He simply had to find it, and that shouldn't be too hard. It

was noisy, after all. And maybe *this* stream led to that one! He remembered that the bearded man angled away from Pine Lake Creek to reach this valley. So maybe this stream didn't meet it. But it didn't matter. During the scramble through the woods, Carlos heard its burbling to his right, until it faded from his hearing. "Which means I gotta go left to find it once I leave the valley."

Carlos suddenly felt confident and strong. He knew how to find his way back! He reached a steep rise and fought his way up, clawing at rocks and roots with his hands and feet, like a cat climbing a tree. But his burst of energy soon faded, leaving weak and shaky muscles behind. And he nearly slammed his head against a boulder. "Slow down, dope!" he gasped as he reached the top. He flopped down and sucked in air.

The boy tried to rest his left hand on the ground, but there was no ground to rest it on! He toppled sideways, and only a wild grab at a tree root saved him from falling. He was inches away from a long drop-off. He could barely hear the stream trickling far below.

He gave himself a while to rest and calm down, then began a slow, careful mix of walking and crawling. He wanted to get back to camp as soon as he could, which made this pace *maddening*. But it was better than falling off a cliff.

* * * * * * * *

They'd been rolling over smooth road for a while, though it wasn't quite concrete. Gravel, maybe. Mashell even managed to fall asleep. But she was awake now. Something jarred her.

The pickup thumped and rocked its way down and up a ditch. The others jerked awake. "What's goin' on?" mumbled Bronce.

Mashell glanced out the narrow side window. It was too dark to see, but branches scraped the outside of the topper with grating squeaks and whaps. "We sidetrackin' into the woods again."

Anna let out a soft moan. "Where's he taking us?"

They wouldn't find out for a while. This was the roughest part of their journey so far. Mashell could barely keep her head from slamming into the walls. At times the rear tires left the ground. And they always came down with teeth-rattling *whumps*.

She felt battered all over. "This—how he gonna—get—rid of us?" she yelled. "By *jarrin'* us to—death?"

Terror had never left Anna's eyes since the bearded man first grabbed Mashell. "Please don't—talk like that," she begged.

"I'm sorry, girlfriend. I don't mean to—crack—mean jokes. I'm—scared too."

"We gotta pray! We just—gotta pray!" Anna made the sign of the cross on herself, though she looked like she was directing an orchestra because of the truck's bobbing and swaying. She clapped her hands together, shut her eyes tight and poured out fast whispers.

Mashell joined her, silently. *Don't let him kill us. Please, Lord?*

Neither boy said anything, but Mashell watched Felipe cross himself, too.

The ground seemed to smooth out a little and the branch scraping stopped. A clearing? A trail? She couldn't tell.

Then the pickup slowed and stopped, though the man kept the engine idling. Mashell stared out the window and thought she could make out a large clearing surrounded by trees. A meadow maybe, like the one back at camp. If she—and the others—were only back there!

The man hurried past the window, so close he nearly brushed it with his shoulder. She pulled back with a grimace. He dropped the tailgate and ordered them out and Mashell's heart began to pound. *This is it! What he gonna do?*

Nothing. He did nothing. Except to slam the tailgate shut, stride to the front of the truck and hop back in the driver's seat. It was rolling forward before he even got the door closed.

Mashell screamed and chased after him. *"No! Don't leave us alone out here! Don't leave us!"*

The man gunned it and the truck lurched forward, spitting grass and dirt from under its tires. He made a wide circle, jounced back onto the track and roared away.

Mashell didn't stop running until the taillights disappeared. Then she bent over and clutched her knees, calling him as many nasty names as she could think of. "Low-down coward! Snake! *Slime ball!*"

The others were just as upset. "I can't *believe* it!" yelled Bronce. "Why he just *leave* us? An' why *me?* I *did* my job!"

Mashell glowered at him. "Because of *you* we in this fix!"

"It ain't *my* fault you got caught spyin' on me!" he shot back.

"Drughead!"

"Cow!"

Anna cut them both off. Now that the bearded man was gone, she seemed much less afraid. Much stronger. "Stop it, both of you! Getting into a fight isn't going to help anything! I'm *glad* he's gone! I thought he was going to shoot us! Now we can find our way back to the highway and get help!"

"Unless he's got a partner around here," said Felipe.

The argument was instantly forgotten. They moved close together without realizing they were doing it and stared around with wide eyes, listening with all their might for footsteps.

But the meadow was empty of anything human. No buildings. No fences. Not even a signpost anywhere.

Mashell took a deep breath. "I think we alone."

She could feel the others relax. Except Bronce, who was staring at his feet. He looked at Mashell and his eyes were wet again. "You right. I'm the reason we in this trouble. I'm sorry I'm puttin' you all through this."

The girl didn't know what to say. She couldn't tell him "that's okay" because it *wasn't*. "I'm sorry I yelled at you," she finally muttered. It was time to change the subject. "How we ever gonna find the road?"

"Follow the tire tracks," suggested Felipe.

Bronce was clearly angry with himself, which made him frustrated with everything else. "With *what!* Our *noses?* We can't see 'em good enough in the moonlight! You *know* he didn't drive straight! The way he kept turnin', we'll lose the tracks in five minutes!"

Felipe didn't argue with him. He simply pulled his flashlight out of his pocket and turned it on.

8

Carlos was exhausted. He'd left the valley behind and had been hiking for *hours,* it seemed. Why couldn't he hear Pine Lake Creek? Had he missed it? Or gone the wrong direction? Maybe it didn't come out this far from camp.

He wished he was a squirrel, so he could eat acorns. Any food sounded good right now. And his mouth and throat were so dry it was hard to swallow.

He was getting sleepy too. *Maybe I should rest inside a hollow tree.* But what about Anna and his friends? He had to get help! He had to keep going! Besides, he didn't like the thought of crawly things crawling all over him. And what if a bear came along and wanted the same space?

The boy made himself move, though his legs hurt so badly that he almost needed to lift them with his hands. His feet felt like concrete blocks. He was stumbling a lot more and it was getting hard to think clearly.

He was about to plop down on a patch of bare ground when the slightest hint of a sound made him strain his ears. A faint whooshing, like a breeze playing through leafy branches. But the air was completely still.

A burst of adrenalin woke him up. He *knew* that sound! Or hoped he did, anyway. It was too far away to tell clearly. He walked as fast as the darkness allowed and as he neared it, the noise turned into the sweetest music he'd ever heard: the chuckling splashes of the creek.

The sound reminded him of his thirst. "It's okay to drink, isn't it?" He reached the bank and bent to touch the water. It was *cold* on hands that were already almost numb. But he scooped some to his lips, anyway.

It was *delicious*. It didn't have any taste at all, actually. He filled his palms again and again until his stomach was full of water and his hands were *freezing*.

"I wish I could drink this stuff all the time!"

He hiked alongside the brook, wondering how long it would take him to reach camp. The moon had gone down by now, the stars looked faint and small and he thought he saw a patch of lighter gray sky coming up over the mountains. He could see more clearly, he was certain of that.

Carlos suddenly felt warmer. Flushed with heat, in fact. He nearly unzipped his jacket. But then the heat went away and a wave of cold took its place. It was followed in another moment by heat again.

He slowed down. His stomach was starting to hurt. *Really* hurt. Like a gang of mouse-sized karate experts was kick-fighting in his abdomen. He doubled over, then sank to his knees. *"What's going on?"* he cried out.

He felt too weak to move. The pain grew until it felt like the kick-fighters were using torches. He lay down on his side and rocked slightly, whimpering.

What had made him sick? The *water?* Maybe he was *dying*. With pain like this, he almost hoped so.

* * * * * * * *

It didn't take them long to lose the tracks, even with Felipe's flashlight. The pickup had gone over ground no one else had driven on. Some of the tall grass had recovered enough to partially stand again. Some of it was lying down for other reasons. Other trails led them astray too—made by animals, Bronce told them. He'd hiked in wilderness before.

Grogginess hit Mashell even harder now that she was stumbling around in the dark and the cold. "Give it *up,*" she kept insisting. "Wait 'til daylight."

She didn't have to argue much. The others were just as tired. "But what if a bear finds us?" Felipe asked her as they stretched out around a tree at the edge of the meadow.

"He just gonna have to keep his snorin' *down.*"

Grass tickled her face and hands and it was hard to rest without a pillow. But exhaustion overtook her.

She jerked awake in what felt like the next second and opened her eyes to yellow-green and tan grass and a tiny purple flower inches from her nose. Birds were singing. The sun was up.

Its rays weren't giving off much warmth, yet. Mashell sat up shivering and rubbed her hands together. Her stiff muscles complained sharply at having to move, especially her upper arms—from the canoe races. She shook her head. Yesterday's camp games seemed like they'd happened years ago. The girl wondered when they'd make it back to Pine Lake. She didn't let herself wonder *if*.

Anna was awake too, and she stood with a gasp of pain. "I'm so *sore!*"

"Me too, girlfriend! An' I *hate* bein' cold!"

The boys groaned and lifted their heads, looking as bleary-eyed and rumpled as she felt. And she was absolutely *starving*. "Anybody got a snack on 'em?"

"We'd have ate it a long time before this," answered Bronce.

Felipe started to talk about what the Bible camp was probably having—pancakes with maple syrup or bacon and eggs and hash browns. The only one who didn't order him to *shut up* was Anna.

They had no choice but to start walking. "Can't even wash my face!" groused Mashell. "My eyes feel like I got sandpaper glued to my lids."

Felipe seemed determined to look at the bright side. "At least we didn't get eaten by a bear!"

"I hope Carlos is okay," said Anna.

They found the tire tracks again, in the woods' softer ground with its layers of brown leaves and pine needles.

Walking loosened her muscles and lifted Mashell's spirits a little. If only they could find water!

As if in answer, her ears caught the whispery sparkles of a distant brook. Bronce insisted they leave a marker. "We'll never find the tire tracks again if we don't. If you think we can walk straight back to this spot through this thick woods without somethin' to go by, then you never spent any time in the wilderness."

They hadn't, as a matter of fact.

The four kids emptied their pockets and came up with two used tissues, a comb, a crumpled wrapper from a chocolate bar (which made Mashell's mouth water) and Felipe's flashlight.

Its neon-orange plastic was the only thing bright enough to catch their eyes from a distance. So he reluctantly left it standing on a flat-topped boulder. Mashell kept glancing at it over her shoulder as they headed toward the stream. It was alarming how quickly the flashlight blended into the backdrop of leaves and branches and tree trunks. And how alike all the bushes and rocks looked. She hoped they'd find the tracks again, even *with* the marker.

They neared the creek and her thirst grew more with each step until she broke into a run, leaving the others behind. She reached a place where it bubbled over a log in a miniature waterfall and formed her hands into a bowl. The water quickly filled her palms, icy cold and as clear as tap water. Mashell could hardly wait to taste it.

"Hey, don't drink it!" Bronce ordered her sharply.

She paused with freezing water dripped down her arms and soaking her jacket sleeves. "Why *not?*"

"You gonna get as sick as a dog—from *Giardia.*" (Pronounced jee-AHR-dee-uh.)

"Gee-what's-a?"

"Giardia! It's a teeny little parasite—you can't even see it—that gets carried along in the water from off of beavers and otters and things. You drink water that's got it in there and you'll get the worst stomachache you *ever* felt. Diarrhea, too."

She emptied her hands. "How do we know if there's that *whatever*-you-call-it in *this* stream?"

"You gotta figure that it's in any water anywhere in the wilderness. You never *ever* drink water from a stream or a lake or nothin' 'til you boil it. Or put it through a filter you can buy that gets rid of the giardia."

Mashell glared at him. "Who *says?*"

"Stan told me 'bout it yesterday! I asked him if I could get a drink from the lake."

"I don't suppose you got one of them filters on you!"

"I wish I did."

She was getting angry again. "You mean to tell me I gotta stand here thirsty enough to choke and listen to this water runnin' and I can't get a *drink?*"

Bronce shrugged. "Not unless you can figure out a way to boil it."

"Yeah, right! I'll rub two sticks together to start a fire an' then I'll heat the water in a rock!" Her voice rose. "What'd you have us leave the tire tracks for, if we can't drink the water?"

"You said yourself your eyes feel like sandpaper. We can wash off."

How frustrating! She slapped the water on her face and rubbed the sleep out of her eyes. But not having a towel meant her skin had to drip-dry, which made it feel tight enough to rip apart when she smiled. And she desperately wanted to let the drops trickle into her mouth instead of blowing them away.

What if he was wrong? Why should she endure thirst when relief was bubbling at her feet? She scooped another handful with a defiant glance at him. But he wasn't drinking it and neither were the others. She hesitated. What if he was *right?* It was bad enough to be left in the wild. She didn't need to be violently sick.

The girl nearly tossed the water at him instead of pouring it back in the brook. *It's your fault we in this fix!* But she didn't say it out loud. Why start another fight?

They headed back to the tire tracks with Bronce leading the way. Felipe's flashlight seemed to have disappeared and only Anna's sharp eyes kept them from missing the tracks themselves. Felipe insisted they follow them backwards until they found the light. "It's brand new! I'm not leaving it!"

"We might as well go back where we started from an' just stay there," muttered Mashell. But she kept her eyes peeled and was the first to spot the flashlight, still standing on its rock like a tiny lighthouse. Now there was nothing left to do but trudge. On and on, staring at the faint grooves a truck-width from each other and hoping they'd remain visible. The sun grew warm and filled the woods with a patchwork of yellow light and green shadows.

Bronce led the hike, then Felipe and Anna and Mashell. Flies came out and buzzed her head. Mosquitoes lurked in the shade, humming around her ears until Mashell's arms ached from slapping them away. And no one had any bug spray.

Anna nearly walked into a fat spider. Mashell noticed the web first, then the quarter-sized tenant in the center, hanging upside down, rust colored and fierce looking. But Anna was staring at the tire tracks. She was two feet away from having the spider in her *hair.*

Mashell darted forward and shoved her friend sideways. She cried out in surprise and disgust. "Wha—why did you *push* me?" It took a lot to make Anna angry. Mashell simply pointed at the web, which drew a scream from Anna. Bronce whirled around and shouted in fright, "Where's the *bear? What's goin' on?"* Anna showed him and he raised his eyebrows and whistled. "Yeah, I wouldn't want that big ol' thing crawlin' around on *my* head."

They reached another clearing and the tracks disappeared. They divided the meadow into sections and searched every inch of it. With a sinking heart Mashell suggested they look all around its edge and on into the woods beyond.

No sign of them. She was about to give way to despair when she heard a distant noise: thump-a-*thump*, thump-a-*thump*, thump-a-*thump*. The others were staring in its direction, too. What made it so familiar? It's *rhythm*. She'd heard that pattern somewhere before, but she couldn't place where. "It goin' too fast for a *bear*, ain't it?" she whispered.

It was coming toward them through the woods. Suddenly the pattern changed to steady, rapid thuds. Then it slowed to swish-a-swish-a-swish. By then she'd guessed what was making the noise, and she wanted to squeal with joy and jump up and down.

A chestnut-brown horse walked into the clearing. The kids cheered and waved at its rider, a young man dressed in a park ranger's uniform—forest green pants, a gray shirt with an arrowhead-shaped national park patch on the upper arm and a brown hat that looked exactly like the one worn by Smokey the Bear. He reigned his horse to a stop and stared at them in surprise. *"Hello!"* he called. "Are you kids camping with your parents?"

Mister, your guess ain't even close! thought Mashell.

Carlos had never known such misery. On top of the pain, he was *sick*. His intestines would feel like they were twisting and jumping and he'd have to scramble behind the nearest bush.

When the attack of diarrhea was over, all he could do was lie on his side and moan. His body shook and he was covered with sweat that only made him feel colder. He wanted *Mama!* He wanted to feel her gently stroke his face and tell him in soothing tones that he'd feel better soon. He wanted her to bring him broth and crackers and whatever else she always gave him when he was sick.

And he wanted to be lying in his own bed, wrapped in blankets, instead of on hard ground with leaves and pine needles in his face.

The sun had been up a while. Between attacks he felt a little better and managed to walk with dragging feet, letting the stream guide him. He was as thirsty as ever, but he wasn't *about* to drink any more water!

He couldn't have cared less about bears, now. *Let* them eat him! The only thing that kept him moving was concern for his friends and Anna. *I've gotta get to the police!* he told himself with gritted teeth. And so he plodded on. Until a wave of heat passed over him and those kick-fighters started up again.

By midmorning he could barely walk. His skin felt tingly and his ears were filled with a roaring sound. The attacks had subsided; his body had nothing left to get rid of. He felt dizzy and fell without tripping over anything. And there he lay, near a patch of thick bushes, until restless sleep filled with strange dreams came over him.

He awoke with a jerk. Had he heard something? His head felt like it was rotating. So did the ground. The bushes looked as large as elephants and the pine trees as tall as mountains. His ears still rumbled and the creek sounded like it was a raging flood, but he could still make out an approaching sound: low-voiced animal grunts and the crackle of something pushing through the underbrush.

A bear was coming. This was it. He was about to be eaten, and he was too weak and dizzy to get away. Carlos covered his head, curled in a ball with his eyes tight shut, and waited for the first bite. The bushes shook as though the bear was trying to uproot them. Its rapid footsteps made the ground tremble. Closer and closer, until he felt its breath hot on his neck and arms. He began to whimper. He couldn't help it.

A paw scraped his back and head and the bear gave out a long, low moan. Then its voice went into high, broken whines that ended in the most beautiful sound Carlos had ever heard—a *bark!*

His eyes shot open and he rolled over, ready to hug the dog someone had sent to rescue him. He would have cried out in joyful surprise if the animal's tongue hadn't slapped him in the mouth. The boy giggled through pursed lips as the tongue hit his face and throat and ears. He wrapped his arms around the wriggling body, pressed his head against the furry side and was finally able to get a word out.

"Peppy!"

* * * * * * * *

Rescue workers carried Carlos back to camp on a stretcher, with Peppy trotting happily beside his head. They only had half a mile to go. When they told him that Anna and his friends were safe and on their way back too, he could have done a cartwheel for joy. If his stomach hadn't felt like it was spinning already.

The other campers stood in a cluster at the edge of the woods. They broke into loud cheers when his stretcher came in sight and wanted to hear all about his escape from the drug dealer. Weak as he was, he would have told them the story if Mr. Hansen hadn't ordered them aside.

They put him in the one guest cabin that had its own bathtub. This was one of the few times he *wanted* to take a bath, but he felt so shaky that he wasn't sure he could. Stan stationed himself outside the bathroom door, ready to help if Carlos needed it. And Peppy sat panting beside the sink, never taking his eyes off his young master.

In spite of trembling legs and arms that felt about as strong as his baby sister's, he managed to climb in the tub. *Oh!* Warm water and soap bubbles reached nearly to his chin, soothing away the chills and the dirt he'd been living

with for nearly twelve hours. "Peppy, do you suppose
they'll let us take baths in Heaven?"

His dog answered with a whining yawn.

His clean pajamas felt nearly as good as the smooth
sheets on the bed. He had it all to himself and it was
enormous! Even bigger than the bed he shared with Luis at
home. The boy snuggled the blankets around him and sank
his head deep into the pillow.

He would have fallen asleep if his intestines hadn't
started squirming again. He heard a knock on the cabin
door and Mr. Hansen entered, followed by a pudgy, gray-
haired man dressed in polyester slacks and a golfer shirt. A
doctor, the camp director said.

The doctor stared hard into the boy's eyes. Then he
jammed his huge thumb against his eyelid and pushed up.
Carlos tried to sit still, but it felt like the man was trying to
shove his eye out of its socket. He did the same thing to
the other lid, then rested one arm across his bulging
stomach and the other under his chin.

"Drank a lot of untreated water, did you?"

The boy felt confused. "I dunno. I drank from
the creek."

"How much? A cup? A quart?"

"I just kept scooping it up in my hands. I was really thirsty. I could hear the water sloshing around in my stomach afterwards."

"Mm-hmm. Giardia." The doctor gave Mr. Hansen a knowing look, then pulled a prescription drug bottle out of his pants pocket. "I figured it would be. Give him one of these three times a day for five days."

Five days! "Am I gonna have to stay in *bed* all that time?" Carlos blurted out.

"Not unless you feel like it. These pills'll get rid of the parasites that are playing around in your intestines. You should be up and about again by tomorrow." He winked at Carlos and slapped the boy's shoulder with the back of his hand. "Don't want to miss any fun, do you?"

"No, I don't!"

The doctor gave him a pill and a glass of water and watched intently as Carlos choked it down. He *hated* swallowing pills! But he hated diarrhea worse. Then the man gave him a grape sucker, patted his shoulder again and left. The boy felt insulted. He wasn't a little kid! But he had the sucker reduced to a razor-thin piece of candy glass

by the time Mrs. Hansen arrived with a bowl of chicken rice
soup, crackers and Jello on a lap tray. As hungry as he was
and as good as the food tasted, he ate cautiously. Would the
giardia attack again?

So far so good. He was slurping the last of his soup
when Anna, Mashell and Felipe burst in the room. They
squealed and yelled *"Hi!"* and gave him high fives. Anna
hugged him nearly as hard as Mama would. Then she
caught sight of the dog lying near the bed slapping the floor
with his tail, and her mouth dropped open in shock.
"Peppy! How did *you* get here?"

"There were lots of volunteer people called out to find
us," Carlos explained. "One of them was a rich guy who
owns his own airplane. He was gonna fly somewhere and
bring back a search dog but Stan and Miss Lindstrom told
him that Peppy was really good at finding people and he
could *for sure* find me. So the pilot went all the way to L.A.
and got him! He said it doesn't take that long in a plane."
Carlos stretched his arm down and scratched Peppy's ears.
"How did you like flying, huh? Was it fun?"

The others surrounded Peppy and overwhelmed
him with pats and rubs. He looked into their faces and grinned.

"So how did they find you?" Carlos asked Felipe.

"One of the rangers from Yosemite National Park was following the drug dealer's truck tracks 'cause he thought the guy was a poacher and he'd shot a bear or something. And he found us instead!"

Mashell chuckled. "You shoulda seen his face when he saw us! He 'bout fell off his horse! Really nice guy. Didn't waste no time callin' somebody to come pick us up. He let me talk into his walkie-talkie, too." She gazed at Carlos' empty dishes. "You got anything left? We *starvin'!*"

He shook his head. "Sorry. Hey, where's Bronce?"

"He in *big trouble,* man! There's some cops comin' for 'im."

"Is he gonna get *arrested?*"

The others shrugged and looked somber. "Guess he deserves it," Mashell said. "But I feel bad for 'im. What would *I* do if some drug dealer offered me two hundred dollars?"

"I'd tell him to get lost in the woods!" burst out Anna, fiercely.

Mashell raised her eyebrows at her. *"Easy,* girl! I ain't gonna carry drugs for *nobody!"* She sighed. "I hope Bronce

don't wind up in jail. He kept me from drinkin' water from
that brook, you know. Or I'd have got as sick as Carlos."

He made a face. "You wouldn't have liked it!"

The door opened and Mrs. Hansen, Becky Lindstrom
and Stan hurried in followed by a crowd of kids carrying
chairs, a folding table, and best of all, covered trays. Warm
food smells filled the room: more soup, toast with peanut
butter and something strawberry.

"Yes!" exulted Mashell and Felipe.

The room was now filled with noise and bustle.
Everybody wanted to pet Peppy. (He gladly let them do it.)
Everybody asked questions. Everybody wanted to hear the
lost kids' stories. Daniel Boone lectured Carlos on the
dangers of drinking untreated water—as if he didn't *know.*
The talking grew louder and louder until the door opened
again and Bronce slowly walked in ahead of Mr. Hansen.

Instant, uncomfortable silence.

The sixth grader's face was streaked with tears and he
couldn't look anyone in the face. "Nathaniel needs to eat
too," Mr. Hansen said quietly. "Why don't the rest of you
leave now and let these young people get a meal in. Thanks
for your help. You can hear all about their ordeal later."

He herded the crowd outside. Carlos winced in
sympathy at the horrified or indignant stares the younger
kids gave Bronce as they passed him. No amount of money
was worth that kind of humiliation!

The adults finished setting up the table and dishing up
the food. Then the five kids were left to themselves. The
girls tried to act normal—chatting as they ate, trying to find
things to laugh about—but they soon gave it up to the
almost wilderness quiet that settled over the room.

Bronce was nearing his last bite when the wetness he'd
been trying to blink from his eyes overflowed. He coughed
and shook his head and grabbed a napkin to blow his nose.

"I'm-I'm gonna have to go back to L.A. as soon as the
cops—get here," he mumbled. His chin was starting to
quiver and he clamped his lips together, still fighting not
to cry.

"We're sorry you're in trouble," said Carlos.

"*Why* didn't I tell them dealers in Watts to smuggle their
own drugs?" His voice grew louder. "Now I gotta go on
probation! Now my whole family's gonna be investigated
by some juvenile officer! They might even take me away
from my home!"

His words gave way as he lost the battle of the tears. Anna scurried to grab a box of tissue beside Carlos' bed. She gave Bronce a handful, then patted his back the way Mama did whenever any of her boys cried.

"You want a drink of water?" Mashell asked him, picking up his empty milk glass. "Sometimes that helps me when I'm havin' a hard cry."

He shook his head. "No-th-thanks. Man, I really feel *stupid."*

"Nah!" chorused the others.

Felipe added, "You don't need to. We've all cried about *something."*

Carlos decided to risk sharing a secret. "I did just last night. When I was left alone in the woods, you know? I'm telling you, I've never been so scared! I sat there blubbering like a baby."

Bronce managed a smile. "You mean like me just now?"

Carlos shrugged because he couldn't think of anything safe to say.

The smile didn't stay on the sixth grader's face for long. "I wonder what's gonna happen to me."

"We'll pray for you." The words popped out before Carlos had a chance to think about them, but he was glad he said them. Especially since the others nodded.

Bronce's eyes moistened again. "You can go ahead, but I don't think it'll do any good. You think God wants anything to do with *me,* after what I did?"

Mashell glared at him. "He cares about you! If you think you gotta be perfect for Him to love you, then we *all* in the hurt bag! I did somethin' I coulda got arrested for, too. An' I told myself, *'Girl,* you blew it now! God's mad at you and He gonna stay that way forever!' "

She paused, and Carlos watched her grimace as she remembered something unpleasant. "But then Mrs. Joyce told me that Jesus found a way to handle the problem. You know how He died? They hung 'im up on the cross with nails in his hands an' feet? Well, He did that so us humans could say we sorry to God for doin' wrong—an' we *all* done somethin' wrong *sometime.* Mrs. Joyce says we only gotta do one little sin our whole lives an' as far as Heaven goes, we *out.* But see, when we *do* ask God to take our sins away in Jesus' name, then God says, 'I forgive you! My Son Jesus already took care of it for you.' "

She broke into a warm smile. Bronce stared at her without arguing. He seemed to clutch at every word she said. "I'm sorry, all right," he mumbled. "An' not just

'cause I'm in trouble. I been feelin' bad about this ever
since I told those dealers in Watts that I'd take their dirty old
drugs out here to the wilderness. I keep wonderin' what's
gonna happen to the people that get high on the stuff I
smuggled. What if they die? What if they have a car
accident? What if they beat their kids up 'cause they too
strung out to know what they doin'?"

Silence took hold again. Carlos had no idea what to say
because Bronce was right. Once the cocaine reached the
streets of Fresno or whatever town it was going to, it would
cause harm—wasted money, damaged brains, wrecked
lives.

An idea hit him. "Let's pray that those three packages
never make it, you know! Pray that the cops get hold of it
or that the plastic leaks in the rain and the stuff gets
all ruined!"

Mashell chuckled. "How 'bout that the smuggler gets a
flat tire, and in all the bouncin' and jouncin', the drugs fall
outta the truck!"

The others picked up the theme and offered every
outlandish idea from the smuggler getting sick from giardia
to the truck going off a cliff. The suggestions made Bronce

grin, anyway. "You can just ask God for stuff like that an'
He'll *do* it?"

Carlos wasn't so sure. "I bet I know what Mrs. Peterson
and Mrs. Joyce would tell us. 'Don't ask God to hurt
anybody 'cause He loves *everybody*.' "

Bronce looked skeptical. "Even lowdown drug dealers
that shoot people?"

"Even them."

"But they won't make it to Heaven, will they?"

"Not unless they become Christians," Carlos explained.
"Like Mashell said, they gotta feel sorry for their sins and ask
Jesus to take them away. And then ask Him to take over their
lives. Make Him the boss, you know? Then, with His help,
they'll stop doing things like selling drugs and shooting people."

Bronce took a moment to ponder what Carlos was
saying. "Can anybody become a Christian?"

"Yeah," answered the other four kids at once. "We all
did," continued Mashell.

"I think I'd like to become one, too."

Carlos grinned. He would have offered to help Bronce
pray if the door hadn't swung open and two uniformed
police officers hadn't walked in.

One was a woman. She seemed taller than any other
lady he'd seen, probably because her dark blue uniform,
complete with a badge and a holstered gun at her side, made
her look imposing. Neither officer smiled as they led
Bronce away. As he reached the door, he gave his new
friends a last look. His eyes were dry, filled with worry and
misery.

"See you in a few days," said Anna softly. "We'll pray
for you."

Carlos added hurriedly, "You can do what we said
anytime. Just talk to Jesus, you know? He's always around,
and He's always listening. He's the best friend in the
universe."

Bronce nodded. Then he was through the door
and gone.

10

The next morning Mashell groaned as she crawled out of her tent. The ground felt harder every time she slept on it. Why couldn't she have gotten just a *little* sick, so she could have slept in a cabin like Carlos?

He seemed almost back to normal. He joined them at the picnic tables, though he didn't eat the bacon and eggs they wolfed down. Mrs. Hansen cooked a bowl of hot cereal for him.

As the forty young campers finished eating, Mr. Hansen made an announcement. "Today we're driving you into Yosemite National Park, one of the most beautiful places on earth."

He was cut off by claps and cheers. "We'll give you a tour of Yosemite Valley. Then I've set up an appointment with the park ranger who rescued Anna, Mashell and

Bronce." (She and Anna squealed, which drew a please-stop-interrupting look from him.) "His name is John South and he's a wildlife technician who monitors bears and other big mammals. He'll let us see the equipment and explain how an animal like our raiding bear is drugged and radio-collared."

The man paused and looked at Carlos. "By the way, South himself is the one who shot our black bear with a dart. He told me it hasn't set foot in another camp, yet."

That drew a cheer from Carlos.

They were underway in an hour in four large vans, with the oldest kids and Peppy and Stan riding in the last one. Mashell sat next to Anna, as usual, as the van lurched its way around the mountain road's steep curves. "This ride ain't *nothin'* compared to the one we took in that drug smuggler's pickup!" she boasted to the group. Felipe and Anna heartily agreed.

The view looked the same as the one she saw coming into Pine Lake Camp. What made Yosemite Valley so special? Then she began to see gray mountaintops in the distance. They didn't look as smooth and rounded as the other peaks and they weren't covered with pines. Their sides seemed to rise straight and sharp. But she was too far away to really tell.

The van entered the longest highway tunnel she'd ever seen. Amber lights ran along the top. Its sides were rugged, cut from solid rock. "We're passing right through a mountain," Stan told them.

Strange feeling! "Hope they made the roof supports strong enough," Mashell whispered in Anna's ear. The engine noise bounced back at them, much louder in the tunnel. The far end was a bright dot that grew larger by the second.

They passed through it and the echoing motor roars stopped as though someone had switched off a radio. But that's not what made Mashell gasp and cry out in wonder. A vista spread out before her. The van pulled into a parking stall so the young campers could climb out and join hundreds of other gaping tourists in front of a low rock wall that kept them from falling down the mountainside. Which was good for Mashell. She was so enthralled she hardly looked where she was going.

To the right she saw an enormous, square-topped cliff. "That's El Capitan," Mr. Hansen explained in a loud voice. "It's the largest single rock in the world."

Mashell was amazed. "It's a *mountain,* ain't it? It can't be a *rock!"*

"It's a rock the *size* of a mountain!"

Dark trees—mostly pines—grew up to El Capitan's base, looking as small next to it as grass to a house. The trees covered the valley's curve with a blanket of green. More granite peaks lined the valley—some that rose in columns, some that were rounded on top. A waterfall that had been cutting a wide groove in its path for centuries poured down across the valley from El Capitan. "Bridal Veil Falls," said Mr. Hansen.

The white cascade of water moved back and forth in the wind and a rainbow glinted off its spray. Further down the valley, on the same side as the falls, Mashell noticed a large dome. Only it was cut straight from top to bottom, as though someone had sliced it with a knife. The side that would have fallen into the valley was gone, leaving half a mountain.

"Half Dome," Stan told her. The name certainly made sense.

Mr. Hansen named several other peaks—Sentinel Rock, Cloud's Rest, the Cathedral Spires, the Three Brothers—

until she couldn't keep track of them anymore. She only
half-listened as he explained that the valley had been cut by
glaciers, which was why the mountainsides rose like walls.
She only knew it was the most beautiful place she'd ever
seen.

I always said you were a good artist, she silently told God.

The kids spent the morning riding through the valley.
They ate lunch along the meandering Merced River, then
hiked a mile to the base of thundering Yosemite Falls. It
dropped nearly three thousand feet and its roar made the
brook flowing into Pine Lake sound like a whisper. "Don't
anybody drink the water!" yelled Carlos with a pointed stare
at the kid he kept calling Daniel Boone.

They ended the afternoon with a visit to John South's
office. It was in a small, chocolate-brown building—one of
several in Yosemite Village—that housed four offices. A
wooden sign over its door said "Wildlife Administration."
He met the young campers there, looking as official as he
had when he and his horse found them. Only today his
uniform was crisp and absolutely clean. He wasn't wearing
his ranger hat at the moment. His short, blond hair was
perfectly combed.

To Mashell's delight, he greeted her and Anna and Felipe in front of the others. "But where's the other boy?" he asked with a frown.

"He had to leave," answered Mr. Hansen quickly.

Mr. South cleared his throat. "Oh, I'm sorry to hear that."

He led them from his office to a room further down the hall that he referred to as the monitoring center. Its walls were painted creamy white and they were covered with animal posters and lists of regulations and area maps. He pointed to two long counters running along the outside walls. "Here's where we headquarter our equipment. You can see this place gets pretty cluttered."

He shook his head at the scattered array of wires, paper and coffee mugs between four computer terminals and their keyboards. Mashell noticed a black, portable radio that made her think of Bronce and his precious boom box. She was sorry her new friend was missing this demonstration. *Please let him stay with his family,* she found herself praying.

She forced her mind back to what was happening. Mr. South picked up a large, tan collar with a small, silver, metal box attached to it. "As you kids saw firsthand, we deal as quickly as we can with marauding bears. I happened to be in your area when I got the call that a bear had broken into one of your tents." A sparkle entered his eyes. "Whose was it?"

Carlos and Felipe raised their hands.

"Scare you pretty good?"

The boys nodded emphatically, and the others gave sympathetic chuckles.

"It was an ideal situation for me because I was able to catch him in the act and immobilize him on the spot. This should create a powerful connection in our bear's mind between raiding tents and getting a painful shot in the rump."

More chuckles. Mr. South held up the collar. "After my assistants and I weighed him and checked his health, we put a collar like this on him. It'll send us signals that we can use to locate him until it falls off two or three years from now. We'll know if he enters any more campgrounds."

He picked up an inch-and-a-half-thick rectangle of metal about the size of a jewelry gift box. "The transmitter sits inside this box and it's riveted to a collar; this one isn't attached so you can get a better look at it. Notice the black strip taped to it. That's a magnet. When I remove it, the transmitter will automatically send its signal. I'll let you listen to it on one of our receivers."

The ranger set the collar and the transmitter box on the counter behind him. "Any questions so far?"

Mashell raised her hand. "You in a lot of danger doin' this, ain't you?"

He cocked his head. "Oh, some I suppose, especially if I'm not careful. I was opening the latch on your bear's cage after we'd hauled him about a hundred miles away. He was wide awake and so desperate to get out that he caught my arm when he was pulling himself from the cage."

Mr. South rolled up the sleeve of his left arm. The others "oohed" in sympathy. But Mashell gave a sharp gasp and clamped her hand over her mouth to keep from screaming. She flinched as though someone was about to grab her from behind. The room no longer felt safe.

Mr. South was explaining that he always had a helper back him up with a real rifle whenever he tranquilized bears. But Mashell couldn't listen. It was all she could do to keep from fainting.

The scar he'd shown them was actually two side by side scratches curving down his arm like snakes, one as wide as a magic marker line and the other like a pencil mark, with patches of dried blood on the wider one.

They were the nastiest scratches she'd ever seen. And she'd seen them before.

11

The adults didn't notice Mashell's reaction. But the Good News Club kids certainly did. Carlos and Felipe gave her questioning looks. "What's wrong?" whispered Anna.

Mashell's breath came in gasps as she furiously waved off Anna's question. What was she supposed to do? Announce to the group that the drug smuggler who had kidnaped her and her friends was at this moment showing them how a signal receiver worked?

Mr. South had pulled the magnet off the unattached transmitter box and was letting the young campers listen to its signal on headphones. *Good!* He was busy! He hadn't seen her near-hysterics. She made herself breathe more slowly, then walked as calmly as she could to Miss Lindstrom. "Can Anna and me go to the restroom?" she asked quietly.

"Sure."

A minute later, Carlos and Felipe asked Stan if they could take Peppy outside, and he let them go without noticing who else had left the room, thank goodness. Mashell led them outside at a rapid walk and didn't stop until she reached three pines growing together alongside the gravel parking lot.

"So, what *is* it?" demanded Carlos.

"Mr. South is the man who kidnaped us!"

Mouths dropped open in shock. "No way!" squeaked Felipe. "This guy is blond and that guy had long black hair and a beard—

"Ain't you never heard of people *disguising* themselves?" she interrupted hotly.

"How do you *know* he's the drug smuggler?" Anna asked her.

"That scar on his arm! I saw it that night when he was tryin' to pick up the flashlight an' that backpack he put the cocaine in. Ain't no way two different men are gonna have matchin' scratches like that! They was *nasty.*"

Carlos looked skeptical. "Are you sure? It was getting kind of dark when that guy grabbed us . . . ."

"*Yeah,* I'm sure! I'll never forget those scratches as long as I live." She was starting to shout in frustration.

An adult voice carried toward them. Mr. Hansen. He'd just stepped outside the office building. "What are you kids doing? Stan and Becky told me you asked to use the rest room. You didn't need to, did you?" He began to stride toward them. "If there's anything I require at all times, it's honesty."

Mashell had to make a quick decision. Should she expose Mr. South's crime? But if her friends were this hard to convince, how could she get the adults to believe her?"

She bit her lip and turned toward the camp director, who stopped a few feet from them and folded his arms across his chest. She spoke up before he did. "Mr. Hansen, I *had* to get away from Mr. South!"

The man frowned. "What in the world for?"

"He the drug smuggler! He the man that dragged us off through the woods an' then left us! He held a gun at my *head!*" She began to shake and it was getting hard to breathe again.

His frown deepened. "This is a very serious accusation you're making here. Do you have any proof?"

She started to tell him about the scar. But Felipe cut her off with a voice full of excitement. "Oh! That's how he found us the next day! He didn't just *happen* on us! He knew right where he left us!"

"At least he rescued us," put in Anna softly. Mashell glared at her and she quickly added, "but that doesn't excuse what he did. We could have gotten lost forever."

Mr. Hansen was growing impatient. He held up both hands, palms out, and gave them a stern order. "Everybody stop talking except Mashell."

When she'd finished pouring out why Mr. South needed to be arrested *right now,* he stood in silence, tapping the fingers of his right hand on his chin. "This is extremely serious," he finally muttered. "I don't think it's likely you'd mistake a scar that awful for someone else's. But John South is an excellent wildlife technician who's earned the respect of everybody connected with Yosemite National Park. They can't arrest him—they can't even *accuse* him— of something this terrible without more proof."

He sighed. "I'd better let you talk to the police. Why don't you kids go back inside while I drive to their office. It's right here in the village." He started to walk away but

Mashell clutched his arm and pulled him up short. "Go back *in* there? No way! Don't make us go near 'im again! *Please?*"

He patted her hand and spoke in the soothing, maddening tones of a grandmother quieting a toddler. "Calm down, Mashell. If John South is the smuggler, he has no idea you know his other identity and Stan and Becky and the other camp counselors will . . . ."

She gritted her teeth. "You don't *believe* me!"

"I didn't say that. I'm contacting the authorities, am I not? But you've been through a harrowing couple of days and you may be mistaken."

"I ain't!"

He slipped his arm out from under her fingers. "We'll let the police decide."

"Mr. Hansen," she said as he turned away again. "I really *do* need to use the restroom."

* * * * * * * *

Mashell couldn't stand to look at his face. She stood near the door staring at her feet, with every muscle as tight as piano wire. Meanwhile, Mr. South held up an antenna that was shaped like a two-foot-long "H" lying on its side. As he explained how it worked, his tone was warm and informative. Which only made her more afraid of him.

How could he live a double existence—kidnaper and drug dealer one day and rescue ranger the next—and keep his sanity? What kind of a man *was* he?

She lifted up a constant string of prayers. *Keep us safe from him. Don't let 'im get away. Please get me to the police, quick!*

Every crackle of tires on the lot made her glance anxiously out the window. At last, just as Mr. South was thanking the young campers for being good listeners, Mr. Hansen drove a Pine Lake van to the office building's front door. He shook South's hand, then herded the young campers into the other three vans. He kept Mashell, Anna, Carlos and Felipe with him.

"I need to take care of something with these four," was all he said to Stan. "We'll try to make it back to camp in time for supper. Oh, and take Peppy with you. It would be better if we didn't bring a dog where we're going."

Peppy cheerfully went with Stan, but Carlos didn't look at all happy sending him. They drove to the park's law enforcement center, a building not much larger than the one they'd just left. It was a short ride. *We could just as well have walked,* Mashell told herself. She didn't see any police cars parked in the lot. Just white cars that had "Park Ranger" painted on the side in green letters.

They didn't look like policemen either. They dressed the same as every other ranger. The same as John South. Except they wore handguns in holsters at their sides. One of them, a man of average height with a paunch and a ring of short black hair around his bald head, led them into what he called the "briefing room."

It looked like the monitoring center, minus the computer counters and animal posters. It had a long table in the middle. The ranger sat on a cushioned chair on one side and beckoned the kids and Mr. Hansen to sit on the other.

Except there weren't enough chairs. He saw the problem and hurriedly had extras brought in. Mashell was getting more edgy by the second.

She *had* to get the rangers to believe her! But what if they didn't? What if they refused to accept that one of their own was a drug smuggler? Her mouth went dry and her hands shook so hard she had to squeeze them together on her lap.

The ranger's name was Wallace Semko. His eyes looked kind but they had a sternness behind them that only added to Mashell's nervousness. He listened intently as she explained why she believed John South was a drug smuggler—with the other kids adding comments or filling in parts she'd left out.

He took notes and looked more agitated the more she spoke. "Awful business if this turns out to be true," he muttered. "South has been one of our best bear technicians." Mashell felt gratified that he was taking her seriously, at least.

"You gonna arrest him right away?" she couldn't resist asking.

He shook his head. "No, we're not. Just your word about a scar you think you saw isn't enough proof, yet. No offense, but we need something else to go with it. Some harder evidence."

Frustration and panic began to build inside her. "But what if he gets *away?* What if those three packages of cocaine wind up in *Fresno?*"

Mr. Semko frowned, and his thick eyebrows bunched together. "Did you notice anything else? Mismatched tire tracks or something that we could use to prove he'd dropped you off in the wilderness?"

The kids looked at each other helplessly. "What about that old pickup?" offered Carlos.

The ranger took a deep breath. "It would be great if we could find it. Or a piece of the disguise you said he wore. Or best of all, the drugs themselves. But he's probably got them hidden in some wilderness hideaway. *If* he's the smuggler . . . ."

It was becoming clear to Mashell that he didn't believe John South was the real suspect. She closed her eyes and fought to come up with *something*. A thought hit her and she opened her eyes with a gasp. "What about his findin' us a million miles from nowhere? That's too much of a coincidence, him just stumblin' on us while he was out ridin' his horse. No, he found us 'cause he knew where we were! There can't be two coincidences, can there? That the guy who *happened* to rescue us also had a scar on his arm that *happened* to look like the one on the smuggler's arm?"

Ranger Semko sat buried in thought for a while. Mashell fidgeted with her fingers and squirmed in her chair until the man broke the silence by standing. "I'll be back in a moment. Would you like something to drink?"

A younger ranger, a lady, hurried in with coffee for Mr. Hansen and soda pop in Styrofoam cups for the kids. Mashell downed hers and had the cup torn into tiny pieces by the time the officer came back. He cleared his throat as he walked in the room and didn't sit again. "I've been talking this over with other officers. We all agree that there's a lot to make us suspicious about John South, but nothing concrete that could be used against him in court. So, we can't search his apartment or arrest him."

Mashell's heart sank to her toenails. And she began to feel angry. "But he dragged me through the woods with a gun to my head! He scared us half to death! He...."

The man's eyebrows locked together again. "There's nothing we can do until we find more solid evidence."

Mashell caught the other kids' eyes. She could see they felt as frustrated as she did. Somehow, somebody had to find proof that South was the smuggler. Without getting shot or kidnaped in the process.

12

If Mashell hadn't been so adamant about it, Carlos would have started to doubt that Ranger John South was a cocaine smuggler. It didn't seem to matter what the kids thought, anyway. A whole day had gone by and Mr. Hansen hadn't heard from Yosemite's law enforcement rangers. Which meant they hadn't found more evidence against South.

Carlos and Felipe and Anna and Mashell sat on a long log near the campfire. The nightly sing-along and Bible talk was about to begin. "Looks like South is gonna get away with it," Felipe said glumly. He didn't add "if he's the smuggler" because that would only make Mashell bristle.

She'd taken off her shoes and socks and was rubbing her left foot. "I'll tell you, as sore as I am, I don't hardly even care! Can't believe we hiked all day today, after all we been through. As if we ain't walked in the woods enough!"

Carlos had greatly enjoyed the eight-hour nature hike. He'd started the day with a camp backpack across his shoulders, bulging with a spare jacket, a ham sandwich, an apple, cheese curls and two big bottles of *safe* water. By evening the pack was lighter and his muscles ached so badly he wanted to crawl.

But he'd do it again tomorrow. He was beginning to love this wilderness that seemed vast enough to cover the whole world. Its deep silence didn't bother him anymore. In fact, he'd miss it when he went back to the city. Mr. Hansen told the young campers they could vote on what they'd do tomorrow—canoe, hike or go back to Yosemite National Park. He'd vote for hiking.

Peppy had trotted by his side all day, sniffing and huffing and reveling in the new sights and smells. Mr. Hansen insisted he stay on a leash, which was fine with the boy and the dog. Anything so they could be together. Peppy was lying in front of the log with his head on his paws and his eyes shut, too tired to do much more than tap his tail when his young master stroked his ears.

"Too bad Bronce isn't here," said Felipe. "Maybe he knows something about the smuggler that the police can use."

Carlos held his hands toward the fire's heat. "Yeah, I bet he does. I wonder if we could call him . . . ." His voice trailed away as he pictured his new friend. "At least now we know why he acted so weird the first couple of days here." He whistled. "Thought he was gonna beat us up over that stupid radio. He was just all nervous about meeting the smuggler in the woods."

"With good reason!" added Anna.

Felipe leaned forward to warm his hands too. "I wonder how Bronce smuggled the cocaine into camp. In that big jacket he wore, maybe?"

"I doubt it. He wore it the first night and he didn't act like he was hiding three packages in it. They're pretty big, you know?" Carlos narrowed his eyes and thought hard. "Whatever he hid the drugs in, he would've been pretty nervous about it. Like, he wouldn't have wanted anybody to touch it."

The realization hit both boys at the same time, because they sat up straight and stared at each other. *"The radio!"* yelled Carlos

Mashell stood in excitement. "Oh, yeah! Those packages were just the right size to fit in a hollowed-out boom box!"

"Which explains why it didn't work and why he wouldn't let nobody fix it!" Triumph made Carlos feel warm all over. Who needed a campfire?

Mashell suddenly gripped his shoulder. "An' you know *what?* I saw a boom box in that room next to South's office that looked just like Bronce's! Same color, same make, same *size!*"

The four kids gave each other excited looks. "Let's make sure we talk everybody into going back to Yosemite tomorrow," said Carlos.

* * * * * * * *

The next day was sunny with not much breeze and hardly a cloud in the sky. The camp van roared around one of the dozens of curves in Yosemite Valley. Carlos bent his head back until it was mashed against his shoulders and gazed at El Capitan.

"Would you like to stop and look for climbers?" asked Mr. Hansen.

"Yeah!" the kids chorused.

The van stopped at the nearest parking area and the kids scanned the looming, tan-colored cliff that seemed to stretch up forever. Its height took Carlos' breath away. "Could you imagine *climbing* up there? Using *ropes?*"

Felipe shook his head. "They'd have to be awfully strong. I dunno if *I'd* wanna trust 'em." He squinted. "Hard to believe there could be somebody on the cliff right now."

Anna, who had shaded her eyes, gave an excited gasp and pointed. "There! On that little ledge about halfway up. I think I see a couple guys."

Carlos followed her finger, and after some hard staring noticed two tiny dots of color that could just as well have been lint on a concrete wall. Stan peered through a pair of binoculars. "Yup," he announced. "Two climbers. One's wearing a red shirt and the other . . . purple, I think. They're resting and eating, it looks like."

The thought of eating lunch some two thousand feet off the ground with his feet hanging over a ledge and only a couple of ropes between him and death made Carlos feel nauseous. "How can they *do* that?"

"Speakin' of lunch, let's go eat!" said Mashell.

The vans were underway in a moment, then finally stopped at a picnic area near El Capitan's base. The four kids munched peanut butter sandwiches and apple slices and reviewed, in hushed tones, a plan Carlos had named "Operation Solid Evidence."

"Okay, we ask Mr. Hansen to drop us off at South's office so we can ask him if our black bear has raided more camps. Then, while the rest of us keep him busy with questions, Mashell sneaks in and grabs the radio . . . ."

She finished his sentence for him. "Then I put it under my coat and run it to the nearest bathroom for a close inspection." Her whispers had an excited edge to them. She'd insisted on being the one to confiscate the radio. *"I'm* the one who saw it in his office. An' I'm the one who got somethin' to prove, here. Nobody else saw the scar on the smuggler's arm but me."

Carlos was beginning to have second thoughts. Their plan had sounded so good, so foolproof last night. But now that they were about to try it, it seemed dangerous and foolish. He gave Mashell a worried look. "What if you get caught? What if they accuse you of trying to steal South's radio? Maybe we better tell the police to look at it."

She remained stubborn. "No way! Didn't you hear what Ranger Semko said? They can't touch nothin' without a search warrant. An' if I'm *wrong,* if they took his radio apart and there weren't no drugs in it, then South would know that he was under suspicion. Then he'd get off scot-free for sure, 'cause his guard would be up."

Carlos sighed. Her arguments were certainly logical. But they didn't ease his worries. "I still say you could get caught."

"I *won't.* I'll be real careful."

The plan went well at first. They coaxed Mr. Hansen into letting them stop at the Wildlife Administration building. Mashell stayed with the other young campers milling around the parking lot while Carlos, Felipe and Anna (and Peppy on his leash) hurried to South's own office, one door down from the monitoring center. His window was open, and Mashell edged toward it (making sure no adults noticed her), hoping she could overhear their conversation. She couldn't make out words, but she could hear the anxious questions in her friends' voices. South answered with the soothing warmth of an old professor teaching his young apprentices. Which was enough to make her sick.

She glanced quickly at Mr. Hansen and Stan and Becky and the other camp counselors. They still weren't watching her. The girl dropped behind a large bush growing alongside the building and scooted toward the front door with her shoulder scraping the wall. She scanned the front parking lot. No one was around. She shot from behind the bush, dashed through the door and flattened herself against the wall opposite South's office, just out of his line of sight.

She had to get past him to get to the monitoring center! *Easy, now,* she told herself. *Play it cool, girl.*

Mashell slid her hands along the wall as she inched her way along. Closer...closer.... Carlos stood near the office door. She hissed through her teeth, so softly she wondered if he heard her. But he was ready for her signal. He gave her a quick glance, then hurriedly asked the ranger something about the map hanging on his wall behind him.

His distraction worked. South turned his back to the hallway to point out a landmark and Mashell grabbed her chance. She raced past his door as fast as tiptoes would allow and scrambled into the monitoring center. Its door was wide open and she jumped behind it to catch her breath and take stock of her situation.

Everything was quiet except for the low, steady hum of the four computers. The two counters were as jumbled with wires and electronic equipment as they had been the first time she'd seen them. Her eyes were looking for one thing only: an oblong black radio. Where *was* it? It wasn't sitting on the counter anymore. Somebody must have moved it.

Disappointment wrapped around her as she guessed who did. *South prob'ly took it to the same place he hidin' that old truck of his. Or maybe he smuggled the drugs to Fresno already.*

They were too late! She wanted to put her fist through the door. Instead, she stepped from behind it. *I might as well sneak on outta here an' join the others.*

But footsteps in the hallway made her freeze. She scrambled behind the door again and peeked through the gap on the hinged side. A gray shirt and green trousers rushed into the room. *John South?*

No, another ranger—a middle-aged lady with a thick waist and short, black hair. She hurried to one of the computer printers and tore away the last sheet of a printed stack. The paper had pushed its way across the counter and backed up against the wall, spreading out its accordion folds like a pillow full of air. The woman wrestled the stack into something she could carry, muttering under her breath. "Hokey dot-matrix printer! Why can't we get a *laser?*"

Mashell held her breath to keep from squealing. Because as the ranger flattened the paper folds and pulled them off the counter, the black radio appeared from behind the stack. She rolled her eyes at how close she came to missing it.

To her vast relief, the lady ranger missed her *completely* as she hurried from the room with her eyes glued to the computer copies. Mashell waited until the footsteps faded into another office, then grabbed the radio, slipped off her jacket and covered the boom box with it.

She had to get out of here *now,* before someone else came into the monitoring center. She paused at the door and peered right. Carlos, Felipe and Anna were still talking to South. The hallway went around a corner to the left. The girl chose that direction with fast, silent footsteps.

Now *where* was the ladies' restroom? This was a short hall with not many doors...*there it was!* She pushed through its swinging door and dived into the nearest stall.

The girl didn't dare take time to breathe. To collect her thoughts. To calm down. She had to get this thing open *now*. She let her jacket fall to the floor as she propped one leg on the stool, rested the radio on her thigh and peered at the back. Nothing seemed unusual. She looked at the bottom. *Whoa!* Was there the tiniest hint of a seam running along it?

Her hands trembled with excitement as she turned the radio over. The top seemed to have a seam, too, running along its back edge, hidden to all eyes except those looking hard for it. But the crack was so tight she could barely feel it, let alone pry it with a fingernail or anything else. She scratched at it in frustration.

How'm I supposed to open it? She glared at it with gritted teeth. This *had* to be a fake radio. But she needed *proof.* To add to her agitation, she heard adult shouts drifting past the bathroom window. "Ma-*shell!* Time to *go!*"

Oh, boy! What should she *do?* Show the radio to Mr. Hansen? What if he wouldn't believe that she was only borrowing the boom box for a look at it? *Maybe I'll wind up in a jail cell next to Bronce!*

She had to get it open *sooner* than now!   Maybe there was a hidden handle or something in the back. She stared at it with narrow eyes and a heart that was roaring in her ears. *There!* A small, square lid that she could slide away! Maybe the handle was inside . . . .

No, stupid! That's just the battery holder. But wait a minute! If this was a fake radio, then there wouldn't be any batteries in it. In fact, there wouldn't be a battery holder at all! But removing the holder lid *would* make an opening that could she reach her fingers into. Then *maybe* she could pull the whole back off!

"Mashell! Front and center!" she heard Stan bellow. She didn't have much time! She shoved her fingernail against the raised grooves on the holder lid. *Don't be stubborn! Move already!* With a grunt of frustration she set the radio on the floor, braced it with her knees, and pushed on the lid with both thumbs.

Two things happened at once. The small, flat square popped off and skittered across the floor, out from under the stall door and into the bathroom itself. The main door swung open and Mashell saw green trousers over brown hiking boots. The short-haired lady paused, knelt down and picked up the holder lid. Then, still kneeling, she turned her head and saw Mashell. Her expression turned from surprise to anger.

"What are you doing with John South's radio?" she demanded.

Mashell was too excited to answer her. Puffing up slightly through the square opening where the batteries would have lodged in a real radio, the girl saw clear plastic covering white powder. The *cocaine!*

She stared in heart-pounding triumph, then stood to open the stall door and pour out a rapid explanation to the lady ranger. But she didn't get a chance to talk to her. The woman had jumped to her feet, turned on her heels, and was already out of the bathroom. To Mashell's horror, she heard her mutter as the door swished shut behind her, "Just wait until John sees *this.* "

Panic seized her. The lady was about to alert John South that the very kids he'd kidnaped now knew his double

identity! What should she *do?* Chase her down?
Scream at her? *Don't just stand here, girl!*

Clutching the boom box by the handle, she bolted
out of the bathroom. The lady had rounded the hallway
corner by now; Mashell tore after her praying she could
stop her before she reached South's office.

But disgust made the lady walk rapidly. Mashell
skidded into the main hallway in time to hear her saying
indignantly to John South, "Here's what you get for
trusting these kids. They thanked you for your time and
effort by stealing your radio."

The tense anger that entered his voice turned
Mashell's blood cold. "My *radio!*" He burst from his
office and set his eyes on her. Eyes that had the
ferocity of a cornered wolf in them. Eyes that made her
whimper with terror.

Mashell was *trapped!* John South blocked her way to the outside door and she didn't know where the building's other exit was. He took two steps toward her. "Give me the radio," he ordered her in a voice taut with outer calm and inner rage.

She shook her head and backed up two steps herself. "There's no use running," he continued. "We keep the other outside door locked. Give me the radio."

"Little thief!" spluttered the lady ranger. "I think I'll call the law enforcement people!"

South never took his eyes off Mashell. "No, Janet. Don't do that, please."

The girl wanted to turn and run for her life. But she made herself stand still and think. Anna, Carlos and Felipe stood frozen behind South, fear tight on their faces. "Leave her alone," squeaked Carlos.

At that, Janet lost her temper. *"What? How dare* you! *She* stole his radio and you have the gall to treat John like he's doing something wrong!"

Mashell's head was reeling. Where could she go? How could she keep him from grabbing the radio and maybe *her* in the process? Was he lying about the other exit being locked? She didn't dare test his word. If it *was* locked, he'd catch her for sure. What about help? That was it!

She screamed at the top of her lungs. *"MR. HANSEN! HE-E-E-E-LP!"*

Anna joined her with shrieks piercing enough to shatter glass. South lunged at Mashell. But he never reached her. Felipe wrapped himself around the man's legs and Carlos shoved him from behind. South crashed to the floor with a loud grunt and string of swear words.

"I'm calling the police!" shouted Janet, running into South's office.

The smuggler kicked his legs free and was on his feet as quickly as tiger. He grabbed Felipe by the shirt and probably would have sent him headfirst into the wall if Tom Hansen, Stan, Becky and two other adults from Pine Lake Camp hadn't surged through the door.

"What's going on?" Mr. Hansen demanded.

Mashell held up the radio with the white package showing through the square hole in its back. "The cocaine! I found the cocaine!"

South roared through his teeth and flung himself at her again. Yelling with fright, she ducked through the first door she saw—the monitoring room's—and slammed it in his face. The door handle had a lock button on it. She punched it in with her fist barely in time to keep him out.

Her body was shaking and she whimpered through clamped lips. *He gonna kidnap me again! An' this time, I'll be lost for good! Or maybe he'll kill me and get it over with.*

Why didn't this room have a window? She ran to the counters and scattered the electronic equipment, searching for a weapon. A wire to wrap around his neck? He'd never let her close enough. Could she hit him over the head with a signal receiver? The thought made her feel sick.

She was about to start an all-out cry when screams from the hallway caused her to whirl and stare at the door. South's voice thundered through it.

"*Ma-SHELL!* I'm holding a gun to your friend Felipe's head. Get out here *now.*"

Terror made her stammer. "What you-you gonna do to—me?"

"I'm going to take you and Felipe with me."

"No-o-o-o-o!" She broke into loud wails. But he didn't let her cry for long. *"I said open this door!* Do I have to shoot Felipe?"

She gave the counters one last, desperate look. There must be *something* she could use. *Help me, Jesus! Oh Lord, help me!*

* * * * * * * *

Carlos had never felt so helpless in his life. He'd watched his two closest friends being pushed at gunpoint out of the building and into the smuggler's Jeep Cherokee. All he could do was hold tightly to Peppy's leash. Snarls rattled deep in his chest and South ordered him to keep the dog under control or he'd shoot him.

Anna wept silently as the Jeep pulled away, and Carlos couldn't help but wipe a tear or two of his own. What was going to happen to them? He prayed as hard as he ever had. Ranger Semko and another officer drove up moments later (at Janet's bidding), thinking they were going to scold a kid for stealing a radio and discovering they had a far more serious situation on their hands.

They spoke to each other and into their car radios with grim faces, calling on every officer in the park to begin the chase. The other ranger sped away in the car. Semko questioned Mr. Hansen and Anna and Carlos until he clearly understood what had happened. He chewed the boy out (as if he was all the kids rolled into one) for searching South's property without official permission. Which didn't make Carlos feel any better.

Another vehicle pulled into the lot and Semko jumped in and roared away. Mr. Hansen ordered the kids into the vans for the drive back to camp. But Pine Lake was the *last* place Carlos wanted to go.

"Can't I join the search party?" he begged . "I've got Peppy here. He's real good at tracking lost people. If that guy leaves Felipe and Mashell in the wilderness again, Peppy might be the only one that can find them. He found me, you know."

Mr. Hansen shook his head firmly. "We're dealing with an armed, dangerous man here."

Janet was standing next to him. Carlos watched her eyes grow wet as she shoved her fingers into her short hair and blurted out, "Oh, *John!* What did you do? How could you have gotten mixed up in a *drug ring?"* She gave Carlos a pleading look. "He was so good at his job. Trustworthy. Diligent. He cared about animals. And people. Such a decent person . . . ." Her voice trailed away and she dug a tissue out of her pocket to blow her nose. "Still can't believe it."

Peppy was sitting on his haunches shifting his weight from one front paw to the other. His eyes were bright, his ears were lifted slightly and the rust-blond fur and narrow white patch on his chest stood out in full, feathery waves. Strong, handsome, eager. He seemed to be asking if he could join the search, too.

"He's sure a gorgeous thing," murmured Janet, patting his head.

The boy stared hopefully at Mr. Hansen. He didn't need to convince him of Peppy's abilities. He'd seen that first-hand. The man began tapping his fingers on his cheeks the way he so often did when he was thinking. "I'm going to join the rescue volunteers if the park officials call for us. We could definitely use Peppy." He looked at Carlos with concerned eyes. "But I don't know about bringing you into this ...."

He had to fight not to whine. "But Peppy obeys me the best. And I'll stay in the background. Really I will."

Mr. Hansen took a long time to decide, but he finally let Carlos join the volunteers. Anna insisted on staying by her brother's side and he gave in to her, too. Carlos slapped his sister's hands, then waved goodbye to the other young campers. Some of them looked disgusted at having to go back to "boring old Pine Lake." Others looked relieved, and their expressions said, *Who wants anything to do with a drug smuggler?*

And the wait began. No one could do anything until the law enforcement rangers informed them of developments. The ordeal could be over in a few hours or drag on for days. Everything depended on South. Would he leave the kids in the wilderness again? Or hold them hostage in a building? Or fight it out with the pursuing officers? Carlos refused to think about the other things South could do. *Keep Mashell and Felipe safe, Father God. Please, Lord!*

Volunteers began arriving and the parts of Yosemite
Village not directly involved in tourism turned into bustling
activity centers. Such as the Wildlife Administration building
and the Law Enforcement Center. Rangers were busy
speaking into walkie-talkies and shouting instructions and
gathering equipment. Carlos even watched several trot into
the parking lot on horseback.

It was torture having nothing to do. He wanted to help
but Mr. Hansen told him the best way he could do *that* was to
stay out of the way. Which was *not* what he wanted to hear.

He left Peppy with Anna and wandered into the Wildlife
Administration building, just for something to do. The
monitoring room was deserted and he strolled into it, hardly
noticing his surroundings as a wave of worry swept over
him. What were Felipe and Mashell feeling right now?
What was South doing to them?

His eyes fell on a tan radio collar half-hidden among the
jumbled mess of equipment on the counter. The boy
pictured South holding it up and explaining how he used
collars like it to monitor black bears. Rage swept over
Carlos. How could this man save bears one day and kidnap
kids the next?

He wanted to hurl the collar against a wall. Knock everything to the floor. But he took a deep breath to control his anger and distracted himself by naming what he saw. "Okay, that H-shaped thing is an antenna. That box with the leather strap and the dials on it is a signal receiver."

He placed a pair of headphones over his ears, wondering if he'd get into trouble for listening to a transmitter signal, but did it anyway. Except that the collar's metal box turned out to be hollow. What had South used? Oh yeah! The unattached transmitter.

Where was it? He searched the counters and the floor. He looked behind the stacked-up printer paper. He even peered into a couple of coffee mugs. Someone must be using it.

Janet rushed into the room and he pulled the headphones off with a guilty wince. She raised one eyebrow at him. "Making sure everything works?"

"I—uh—just wanted to hear the signal from that transmitter again. You know, the one that was in a little box that wasn't attached to anything. But I can't find it."

She yanked open the door of a metal storage cabinet and hurriedly pulled binoculars and first-aid kits and other items off the shelves. "It should be right there on the counter," she told him without looking his way. "We never use it for anything but demonstrations." She froze with a flashlight in her hand. "In fact, I know it's there! I used it for a wildlife talk to a bird-watching club not more than two hours ago."

"It's not. I've looked all over."

Janet glanced his way with a frown. "We really don't have time for entertainment right now." But she added softly, as an afterthought, "I'd like to know where it is, though. The thing's not cheap."

Carlos tried to sound helpful. "I hope nobody stole it."

Hold it! What if .... What if *Mashell* had taken it? She ran in this room when South chased her and she spent quite a few minutes in here .... What if she pocketed it in the hopes that someone would *track* her? The ranger had already hurried from the room. Carlos ran after her, yelling with excitement.

14

Mashell slid her hand into her pocket and felt the smooth metal of the transmitter box. She rotated it in her palm until her fingers came across the taped-on strip that she knew was the magnet. Now, to get it off so the transmitter could start sending its signal . . . .

She didn't dare pull the box out of her pocket. South had made her and Felipe sit in the back seat of his four-wheel drive while he kept the radio beside him, in front. He said nothing at all to them, but he kept glancing at them in his rearview mirror. The girl had to keep him from seeing the transmitter *at all costs.*

And she prayed it would work. That its battery was strong. And most of all, that someone would notice it missing and realize she'd taken it.

The transmitter would be no help at all if she didn't get the magnet off *quickly.* It was frustrating work, one-handed. She tried to hold the little box still in her palm while scratching the tape *quietly* with her thumbnail. But its cool metal was slippery and it kept sliding over her little finger and dropping off into her pocket. Once, it nearly popped out onto the seat.

She stared out the window to hide the irritation on her face. If only she could bring her other hand across and reach it in her pocket! But that might look funny. It might make South wonder what she was up to.

Felipe was already curious. "What are you doing?" he whispered.

"Fidgeting!" she hissed back with a frightened glance at South. He was busy steering the Jeep around a steep curve, thank goodness!

The girl knew she'd have to wait until the man wasn't around to show the transmitter to Felipe. It bothered her, knowing her friend was suffering in scared silence without the hope she carried—the hope that this little metal box would lead their rescuers to them. But she couldn't tell him anywhere *near* their kidnapper.

The magnet *still* wasn't off! She clenched her teeth,
trapped the box in the bottom of her pocket and went at the
magnet with her forefinger. *Ah!* One end finally pulled
loose and she quickly yanked the whole thing away. She
hid the magnet in her hand and transferred it to her other
jeans pocket. Now! Was the transmitter giving off its
signal? She'd never know until their rescuers showed up.
Or didn't.

Oh Lord, please make it work.

She was almost upset she'd completed the task because
now her mind was free to focus on the speed race they were
in. South passed every car they came upon as though it was
parked. His tires squealed around curves and Mashell felt
pulled either toward Felipe or the window as though she
was riding a roller coaster.

Felipe suddenly clutched her arm and pointed behind. A
white car with flashing lights on its roof was roaring up to
them! Law enforcement rangers! They gave each other a
silent cheer.

Until John South snaked his way through an "S" curve
that opened out at a wide clearing. Suddenly he veered onto
the graveled shoulder and hit the brakes so hard Mashell

was afraid she'd fly into the front seat. (It was a good thing she and Felipe had buckled their seat belts.)

South yanked the steering wheel and the Jeep jounced across a shallow ditch, over a corner of the meadow and into a thick stand of birch trees. His trick worked. He'd braked on gravel so he wouldn't leave skid marks. He'd turned into the ditch at a sharp backward angle so the tracks wouldn't show to a vehicle traveling the direction he'd been going. Mashell watched in bitter disappointment as the ranger car sailed past their hiding place without even slowing down.

They sat awhile, perhaps as long as half an hour. Two more ranger vehicles whisked by. Their kidnaper finally pulled back onto the highway and drove more slowly this time. They saw no more white cars with thin green stripes on the sides. There was hardly any traffic at all.

Any other time, Mashell would have enjoyed the scenery—silver, almost white granite mountains spread out all around them. The sky looked a deeper, clearer blue than she had ever seen before. But she was too terrified to have her heart lifted by the beauty around her. She would have given anything to be looking instead at the dingy streets and hazy air of Los Angeles.

South turned off the road, shifted into four-wheel drive and crept along a twisting, boulder-strewn ravine with a dried up stream bed running through it. The rangers couldn't possibly follow him here—unless some of them had off-road vehicles as well.

They left the ravine and rocked and bounced through a tangled oak woods. Then across a meadow. Past a small lake. Through a pine forest. And into a narrow meadow hemmed in by mountains. At the base of the shortest peak, Mashell saw a rough-barked log shack, a dilapidated barn and a corral made of old gray boards and bright, tan new ones. A horse looked at them over the fence, swishing its tail and stomping. It was a different animal than South had been riding when he rescued them. This one was rust-colored with a dark stripe running along its backbone.

He pulled the Jeep into the barn alongside a vehicle she'd come to despise: the old dented pickup with its beat-up topper. If only Semko was here to see this! South hopped out and ordered them to do the same. Then he grabbed the fake boom box, yanked its back off and transferred its three white packages into a square leather pouch that fastened shut with a buckled strap. It had a twin attached to it by a long, wide strip of soft leather. She'd never seen saddle bags before so had no idea what they were.

South made the children march into the shack. It was dark inside, and dusty, and void of furniture except for a large metal chest, one folding chair, a card table and a cot. "Sit down and don't move," he ordered them.

The chest was padlocked. He opened it, pulled out three bottles of spring water and handed two of them to the children before opening his and taking a long drink. Then he tossed them two packets of beef jerky and a bag of trail mix.

The meat was so tough Mashell had to pull it free from her clenched teeth with both hands. Usually she would have picked the raisins and dried apricots out of the mix and eaten only the banana chips and peanuts. But she was *starving,* and who knew when she'd get another meal?

"What you gonna do next?" she asked the man, who was stuffing a fistful of trail mix in his mouth. "Drive on?"

He chewed and swallowed before answering her. "There's no more road."

"You gonna keep us here?"

He took another swig of water and walked toward the

door without answering her. "I'll be in the barn, taking care of the horse. Don't leave the cabin. I'll be watching you closely."

"I gotta go to the bathroom," piped up Felipe. So did Mashell, though she didn't say anything.

South gave him a dirty look. "Hurry up, then." He glared at Mashell. "And I suppose you have to go, too."

"Yeah. But *where?*"

"Anywhere in the great outdoors. Only don't wander too far and get right back to the cabin when you're finished. I'll check on you in five minutes."

She didn't like what she heard him mutter as he turned on his heel and headed toward the barn. "I should've brought *two* horses up here."

* * * * * * * *

Carlos flushed with pleasure and pride as the entire crowd of rangers and volunteers clapped and cheered. Janet

had just told them that he'd discovered the missing
transmitter and that there was a strong possibility Mashell
was carrying it. "All wildlife technicians, gather in the
monitoring room for further instructions."

Anna was so excited she spoke much higher than
usual, and she constantly bounced up and down. She
squeezed Carlos' arm and raved, "Look at all those people
and all that equipment! They'll find them for sure! Way
to *go,* Carlos!"

Another ranger, who had been monitoring the chase,
made an announcement. "South's Jeep was last seen
heading north on the Tioga Road. But they've lost contact
with him. They figure he's four-wheeling over some
backcountry track. They're mobilizing helicopters. I told
them about the transmitter discovery and they want all
signal monitoring personnel to gather at Tenaya Lake.
You're to begin scanning at once."

That was all the volunteers and technicians needed to
hear. Engines started up with eager roars. Carlos watched
the horse-riding rangers lead their animals into trailers.
Everyone moved at a run. Everyone spoke at a shout.

Mr. Hansen beckoned him and Anna to his car. The boy clutched Peppy's leash and tousled his feathery shoulders. "We're moving out, dog! We finally get to go!"

* * * * * * * *

Mashell saw her chance and grabbed Felipe's arm before he could leave the cabin. "Delay your bathroom trip a second. I got somethin' to show you!"

He started to come back with "Can't it wait—?" but the sight of the transmitter box sitting in her palm made him end his sentence with a wild shout.

She shushed him fiercely and he continued in a whisper, "Great job! You're really smart! This is gonna lead those police rangers right to us!"

"If they realize it's missin' and figure out that I took it."

A sound at the door made her whirl with a startled gasp. Oh, thank goodness! It wasn't South. Maybe a mouse or something. She shoved the transmitter deep into her pocket and Felipe took his turn in "the great outdoors." Then

Mashell. By the time she got back to the cabin, the man
was waiting for her.

He seemed calm on the outside, and determined and
methodical. But there was something in his eyes. Anger?
Desperation? Fear? She wasn't given much time to think
about it. South gripped her forearm (something she was
used to by now) and walked her toward the door. Felipe
followed at his heels.

The horse was tethered outside the corral, loaded with a
bed roll and aluminum cookware and the saddle bags she'd
seen earlier, hanging on each side of the horse, behind its
saddle. It was clear what the man intended. He was going
to make his escape through the wilderness. And judging by
his grip, he intended to take her and Felipe along.

She wanted to stop. To struggle. To pull away and run.
But what good would it do? He'd tackle her and she'd
probably get hurt. Then he'd make her keep walking with a
harder grip on her arm. And if he really lost his temper,
he'd grab his gun . . . .

The thought made her shudder. They reached the horse
and South ordered her to climb up. "I ain't never ridden a
horse before," she pleaded. He gave her sharp

instructions—something about planting her foot in the
stirrup and hoisting herself up—but she was too scared to
do it right and he wound up shoving her onto the saddle like
a sack of grain.

Whoa! The ground looked horribly far away—far
enough to break bones if she fell off. Which seemed an easy
thing to do, the way her newfound perch rocked and swayed
and quivered. The horse stomped its hind leg and she felt as
though her whole world dipped sideways. "Make it stand
still!" she wailed, taking a death grip on the saddle horn.

South ignored her. Felipe started to step into the stirrup
but the man pulled him away. "Not you."

Mashell's voice came out quivering. "What you *mean,*
not him? You ain't gonna leave 'im by hisself!"

The man pursed his lips and untied the horse. Felipe
gave her a terrified stare and seemed unable to speak. "He
might never get found!" she continued. "He'll starve! An'
he'll be all alone with nobody to protect him from—"

"Be *quiet!*" snapped South. "Move back and give
me room."

She refused to obey until he pulled out his gun and held
it to Felipe's head. She slid backwards and he holstered the

gun in an instant and swung up into the saddle. Mashell
continued to plead. "Don't leave 'im! Please don't!"

South made a clicking noise with his mouth and
the horse started to walk. She turned and watched
Felipe, standing stock still with wet eyes, and her
heart broke for him. What if nobody ever found him?
What a horrible way to die! Alone, starving,
terrified . . . .

She wished with all her soul she could do
something for him. *Wait a minute!* She *could!* She
could *guarantee* that somebody found him! The girl
reached in her pocket and felt the transmitter box—
hard, cool, with smoothed sides and corners that let her
fingers run easily along them. Her hand closed around
it, then locked, motionless. If she gave the transmitter
up, how would anybody find *her?*

She turned frontward and stared at South's back, a
few inches from her eyes, and yearned to know what he
meant to do. Would he kill her? Would he abandon her
again? Maybe he'd take her all the way to Nevada or
who-knew-where. Maybe he'd leave her somewhere
safe, like in a town. He'd bothered to come back and

rescue them the first time he left them in the wilderness, hadn't he? Which meant he wasn't a complete monster.

But now he had no more disguises. Now the whole world knew of his double life. Which kept her coming back to the question she *had* to know the answer to. *Could she trust him?*

She rotated the transmitter in her palm and looked back at Felipe, still standing by the fence. The distance made him look tiny. As vulnerable as a bug on a window. Any number of things could happen to her, some terrible and some good. But as far as she could tell, he faced only terror and starvation.

Mashell pulled her hand from her pocket, aimed for a thick clump of grass and tossed the transmitter into it.

15

Tenaya Lake was the clearest, most beautiful body of water Carlos had ever seen—smooth as a mirror reflecting the sky and surrounded by mountains. But he was too wound up to dwell on it. He and Anna and about twenty other volunteers were clustered around a white truck with green letters on the side that said the usual. "Park Ranger." Janet sat in the driver's seat. She had donned headphones and was staring at a receiver on her lap. Another wildlife technician was holding an antenna out the truck window.

Carlos knew they planned to start slowly driving and letting the antenna send out waves that searched for the transmitter's signal like invisible fingers feeling for something in the dark.

Janet's truck radio squawked and Carlos watched her grab the mouthpiece. Her voice became loud with excitement. "You've picked up the *signal? Where?*"

Whoops and cheers broke out from the surrounding group of volunteers. Anna flung her arms around Carlos and nearly knocked him on his back. And he was too excited to feel embarrassed about it.

Janet scrawled directions then shouted to the crowd, "One of our horse rangers has put the signal within a circle ten miles in diameter. It isn't moving, which tells us South is probably holed up in some hideaway. He's taken the kids into four-wheel drive country, so volunteers, pack yourselves into whatever off-road vehicles we have here." She glanced at Peppy. "And make sure that dog comes along. Okay? Let's *go!*"

Mr. Hansen and Anna and Carlos (and Peppy, of course) rode in the back seats of a huge old Chevy Suburban. The drive along the highway went fast enough to keep Carlos from losing patience. But once they turned off they became part of a bouncing, rocking, painfully slow-moving convoy, working its way along a rough ravine with a dried stream bed running through it.

Janet led them. She had to stop her truck several times and let the transmitter signal guide them in the right direction.

Maddening! The sun was nearing the horizon. At this rate, they'd *never* find South's hideaway before dark.

And then they stopped altogether at Officer Semko's orders, Carlos learned. Apparently the signal was coming from a meadow near some abandoned buildings. Semko was keeping all unofficial personnel away until he and his other officers knew what the exact situation was. Did South have the kids tied up? Was he holding them at gunpoint? Or had he abandoned them?

Carlos hoped with all his heart for the latter. He wanted the smuggler caught, but his friends' safety was most important to him. It was to everyone else, too. And so they waited again. Only being this close to the smuggler's hideaway made the anxiety even worse.

The volunteers passed out sandwiches for everybody, coffee for the adults, and lemonade for Carlos and Anna. Carlos fed Peppy chunks of dry dog food by handfuls, glad he'd insisted on bringing a bag along. The sun had nearly set when the last thing he expected happened. A white ranger truck came lumbering toward them carrying a driver and a young passenger. Felipe! It *had* to be! But where was Mashell?

Carlos felt wild elation tamped down by fear. His best friend was okay! But what about Mashell? Did South take her? Was she *alive?*

Adult arms pulled the truck door open and helped Felipe out. Anna crushed him in another of her Mama-like hugs, then Carlos grabbed both his arms and started to spin him around in a circle. But his friend wasn't sharing his excitement. In fact, he looked on the verge of tears.

He waved Carlos off, then said in a choked voice, "She gave it up for me. She wanted you guys to find me, so she gave it up! Now maybe *she* won't be found."

"Gave what up?" asked Mr. Hansen. But Carlos had already guessed. He didn't need to see the truck-driving ranger hold out the small, silver, transmitter box on his palm. He didn't need to hear that South had taken Mashell on horseback. The look in his friend's eyes had told him already.

Meanwhile, the rescuers wasted no time getting on the move again. Felipe jumped in the Suburban beside Carlos. *"No way* am I going back to Pine Lake, yet!" he'd declared to a volunteer who offered to take him there. Carlos gave his friend a grin and a hand slap.

The old shack and barn were their headquarters, now.
The children arrived in time to see seven rangers on
horseback galloping away, hot after South's trail. A
helicopter roared overhead, flying in the same direction.
Carlos couldn't help but exult. They were *bound* to catch
them, now! He sobered himself enough to pray for
Mashell's safety. And that the ordeal would be over before
nightfall.

* * * * * * * *

She'd tried every method of holding on except the one
she despised the thought of: holding onto South's waist.
She gripped the back of the saddle where it curved up. But
when the horse trotted, the jarring made her feel like her
arms would snap off. Soon she couldn't stand the waves of
pain that began in her shoulders and pooled at her elbows.

She tried grasping the lower edges of the saddle. But
that made her bend forward too much, and her head kept
bumping South's back. *"Hold onto me!"* he ordered her.

Mashell clasped his belt in her hands. But he urged the horse to a gallop and she nearly fell off sideways. With a cry of fright, she wrapped her arms around his waist and held on for dear life. As much as she hated it, it was better than falling.

She was only vaguely aware of the scenery. They were racing through a pine woods along a faint path. Branches brushed her legs and once in awhile South had to duck. Then the evergreens became mixed with leafy trees. Then they entered a stand of birches that soon tapered away to a clearing.

They neared a narrow, burbling stream and South paused long enough to let the horse drink. But he didn't dismount and he refused to let Mashell down. "But I'm so *sore!* Can't I give my bottom a *rest?*"

They were moving at a trot again before she'd even finished the sentence. The ground began to rise and they passed gigantic granite boulders. Soon the horse was picking its way along an angled path that switched directions back and forth up the mountainside. Its hoofs clattered on hard rock and she prayed it wouldn't slip, especially when it passed steep drop-offs, some of them hundreds of feet down.

The sun was nearly gone and its rays lit the layers of mountains around them with a rose-colored glow. Beyond them Mashell caught glimpses of distant flatlands fading to haze at the horizon. She wished she was on a nature hike so she could enjoy the sight.

They *had* to stop with nightfall, didn't they? Climbing a mountain on horseback was scary enough without doing it in the dark. Besides, how much longer could the horse last, straining its way up with a bobbing head and heaving muscles?

Then her ears picked up the most wonderful sound she had ever heard: the harsh roar of a helicopter engine and the buzzing whirr of its blades. Her stiff, pain-filled muscles relaxed instantly and she nearly cried out with joy. She watched South's back twist and almost laughed at the puzzled terror on his face as he stared over his shoulder. He swore, then cried out, "How did they find us so *fast?*"

Mashell knew the answer but she wasn't about to tell him.

The helicopter made a tight circle around them, close enough to set branches swaying. The horse jerked its head, grunted and nearly reared. Then the loud machine pulled up and soared high overhead like an eagle riding a wind current—a constant reminder that the whole world knew

where John South and his hostage were and that help was
on the way.

Mashell didn't realize she was grinning until the smuggler
told her in a surly voice, "Don't get your hopes up. I've still
got you and they can't do a thing about it."

Her smile went away in an instant. The daylight slowly turned
gray. Desperation jarred the girl. *I gotta get away from him if I
wanna get rescued. It's now or never!*

The horse stumbled. Its sides were heaving and its
sweat made Mashell's lower legs wet. *Poor thing! You
tryin' to kill it?*

A wild idea was forming in her head—what if she
jumped off and ran? She could get a good head start in the
time it took him to stop the horse and get down himself. All
she had to do was stall him long enough for the rescuers to
reach them! She let go of his waist, wondering nervously if
he'd say anything.

He didn't, which encouraged her. But the ground was
far away, even if she managed to keep from hurtling over a
drop-off! And she'd land on hard granite! She also had the
problem of bringing one leg up and over so she could slide
down one side. South would realize what she was up to.

And what if she fell under the horse's hooves? Maybe she could slide off the back . . . .

She couldn't give herself much more time to think or she'd lose what little courage she had. She waited until the trail leveled off and widened. Then she shimmied backwards, pushed herself over the saddle back and the bags, took a deep breath and slid off the animal's rump.

The landing jarred her knees and she nearly fell forward. But in the next instant she'd turned and was running all out. She expected to hear the sound of South reining in the horse, followed by pelting footsteps. What she really heard made her stomach twist with fear—the *clop, clop-a-clop* of a galloping horse.

She glanced over her shoulder. The horse was closing in on her and South was leaning out with his arms poised to grab her.

The trail narrowed ahead, with a terrible drop on one side and the sharply-angled mountain face on the other. Mashell scrambled off the path and clawed her way up the slope, clutching at tree roots as though they were ladder rungs.

South halted his horse and was off it in a blink, racing after her. She was appalled at how fast he climbed. Before she could even scream, he'd caught her shirt and yanked her backwards. He wrapped one arm around her waist, pinned her right arm against her back and growled, between pants, "That—was *stupid!* A waste of—time—and *effort.*" He emphasized the word by wrenching her arm up, toward her shoulders. She yelped in pain.

"Now if you want to get *really* hurt—" he shoved her arm up again—"try escaping again. Do you *understand?*"

"Yeah! *Ah-OW!*"

He walked her back to the horse. As she climbed in the saddle (the last place on earth she wanted to be), she caught sight of movement at a curve of the lower trail. A line of things was coming around a switchback. Brown things with light-colored forms on top of them. *Horses with riders!*

She knew better than to yell in triumph, and she didn't have time to, anyway. South jumped on and made his horse gallop in the last direction she ever expected. Toward the pursuers.

* * * * * * * *

Carlos and Anna and Felipe clustered as close as they could get to Janet's two-way radio without getting in the way. They didn't want to miss a word.

"The helicopter's spotted them!" she yelled to the crowd. "Mashell seems fine. She's riding behind South and the pilot says she's looking at him and grinning!"

That made everybody laugh and cheer. Her next report made them hold their breaths. "She's jumped off! She's running away!"

When he heard that South caught her, Carlos moaned along with everyone else. But hope rose again in a moment. "Here comes Semko and the other rangers!"

If there was ever a time to pray hard, it was now.

* * * * * * * *

South stopped the horse at a bend in the trail that jutted out from the mountainside. The rescuers would reach the next curve behind them at any moment. He had switched places with Mashell, so that she sat in front of him. He had a tight grip on her forearm and he held his handgun to her temple.

She could clearly hear the swishes and clicks of the hooves. The snorts. Then coughs and a spoken word or two. Her heart was thudding and she could hardly swallow. This was her worst nightmare come true. So close to freedom and safety—yet as far from gaining it as the earth was from Pluto.

Ranger Wallace Semko was riding the lead horse. He—and the others— stopped in an instant at the sight of South and his hostage. The smuggler yelled, *"Wally,* you should have known better than to bring your team after me. You knew I had a hostage. Now you turn yourselves around and get off the mountain before it gets too dark to see. I'm getting away and if you try to stop me, I'll shoot Mashell."

Semko looked him in the eye for a long moment then said, "I don't believe you'd kill a child."

He gripped her arm tighter. "Then you don't know me very well!"

The officer gave a heavy sigh. "Look, John. You're only digging yourself in so deep you'll never get out. If you give her up and come with me now, I'll remove the kidnapping charges. What do you *want?* A few years in jail or a lifetime?"

"Neither! I *said* I'm getting away, Wally."

"You'll never make it."

"I will with *her.*"

Mashell couldn't stand it any longer. Her lips quivered and giant tears burst from her eyes. *"Please* don't make me go with you no more, Mr. South! *Please?* Lemme go! I wanna go *ho-o-o-me!"*

South bellowed over her crying. *"Give me your horse, Wally! Right now!"*

She continued sobbing while the kidnapper dismounted, pulled her from his exhausted animal, jerked his saddle bags free and made her hustle to a beautiful, golden-tan horse with a blond mane and tail. "My mare's not much fresher than yours," Semko told him.

South made him attach the saddle bags to his mare. What incredible irony! A law enforcement ranger strapping illegal drugs to a smuggler's getaway horse! But the man had no choice. South kept his handgun aimed at Mashell's head.

He made her sit in front of him again. "Go back to where you started, Wally, and call off the helicopter," he ordered Semko. "If you don't, you'll hear a pistol shot echoing through the pines."

Mashell's wails reached their peak at the sight of her rescuers reluctantly riding away. "You'll answer for this in a higher court than any on earth, John!" one of the rangers shouted back at him. "Someday I hope you wind up as frightened as you've made that girl!"

South urged the mare to a walk and they plodded upward, the same awful direction they'd been going for hours. Daylight was fading as quickly as Mashell's hope and courage, and night wrapped the mountainside and her heart in darkness.

* * * * * * * *

Anna broke down in tears at the news. Carlos and Felipe stared at their toes. The only one who maintained any cheerfulness at all was Peppy, who pawed his young master's leg, begging for a back scratch. The boy obliged him without even realizing he was doing it.

Complete darkness had fallen by now. The volunteers lit a fire and sat around it, talking about anything except what was most on their minds. Then they stretched out in sleeping bags or on bed rolls in the shack and the barn.

Everybody insisted that Anna take the cot. They piled up straw and stretched a tarpaulin over it for the boys to sleep on. They were some of the nicest people Carlos had ever met and he knew that all of them would gladly trade places with Mashell if they could. He certainly would.

He lay on the tarp, brushing his fingers through Peppy's fur and picturing her and the smuggler struggling over a pitch black mountain. Or maybe South would stop and let her rest. As if she *could,* with a gun always pointing at her. And he added one more prayer for his friend's safety to the dozens—maybe even hundreds—he'd already lifted up.

* * * * * * * *

It was the worst night of her life. Soon it became too dark for them to both ride the mountain trail safely. South dismounted and led the horse by the reins with one hand and trained his flashlight ahead with the other. Mashell wanted to get down and walk too, but he made her keep riding "so he could keep her in control," he said.

Exhaustion made her lose all sense of direction and logic.
Were they still going up? Or had they reached the top? Had
they left the trail? They weren't looping back and forth
anymore.

Then they seemed to angle downward. But she was too
tired to understand or care. She'd nod off for several
minutes at a time until a sway from the horse or the feeling
she was falling jerked her awake again. "Can't we *stop?*"
she kept begging. "I'm *tired!*"

He never seemed to hear her. Their pace became slower
and slower. The horse had to pause constantly and step
gingerly over logs or roots or walk around bushes and
boulders. The girl was deathly sick of holding herself at a
backward angle.

They were nearly down the mountain. The sky began to
lighten and its eastern edge turned pink. Mashell could
barely see trees spreading out below her. She found herself
waking up as she noticed they were crossing a ridge with
drop-offs on each side. The left side was a cliff that fell
almost straight down—one hundred feet at least—to a
narrow groove filled with gravel and stones. The right side

tapered steeply like a ski slope to level ground some three or four hundred feet below.

She could feel South's tension, which didn't help her own. He was swearing under his breath and finding each footstep painstakingly slowly.

Suddenly the mare stumbled toward the right. South gave a yell and pulled the reins. But he couldn't hold her. She gave a horse-scream as her front hooves dropped over the edge. The reins jerked from his hands and she plummeted down the slope.

The mare tried desperately to stop herself. But a cascade of loose stones and the steepness wouldn't let her, and she wound up half-galloping, half-sliding on all fours. Mashell clutched the saddle horn and sucked in her breath. Her body leaned far back to compensate for the toboggan the horse had become. A moan rose in her throat—the only sound she could make in her terror.

I'm gonna die! I'm gonna die! All her muscles locked in anticipation of getting crushed against a rock or a tree. Or of slamming to the ground sideways. Or of the horse tumbling end over end. Meanwhile, Mashell knew only thudding, skidding, jarring violence as the mare careened downhill.

And then the ground leveled off so suddenly that the girl nearly slammed her forehead against the horse's neck. The mare slowed to a trot. Then she stopped completely, with heaving sides and quivering muscles. "Yo, girl!" squeaked Mashell with a giggle of relief. "You did it! You got us down safe!" She leaned forward to pat the mare's neck. *Ugh!* Her palm wound up drenched with horse sweat.

For the moment she and the mare were the only beings on earth. And they were both alive! But the rattle of falling rocks made her look back toward the ridge. There was South, hot after them. He slid down the ridge like a skier, with his flashlight's beam waving crazily like a spotlight on rough water.

She *couldn't* let him catch them! "Girl, you got any energy left? 'Cause we gotta *go!*" But how did you make a horse move, anyway? She grasped the reins, hoping if she held them up in both hands the way South did, the mare would get the hint.

She didn't move. The man was nearly down the hill! Mashell grunted in frustration. *"Walk,* horse! *Move* it!"

No good. She fought away panic and tried to *think*. What did South do when he wanted a horse to go? What word had she heard him use? *"Whoa!"* she hollered. *That* didn't work! What else? *Oh,* yeah! That clicky sound with his mouth! She gritted her teeth and spit out, *"Kck-kck!"*

The mare took one step. *"Kck-kck! KCK-KCK!"* Two more steps, then she stopped again. Mashell was nearly frantic. South had reached level ground! He was running toward them with murder in his eyes! "Come on, horse! O-o-o-h!"

In her desperation, she bounced up and down and kicked her legs against the mare's sides. The horse began trotting so suddenly Mashell nearly fell off backwards. She caught the saddle horn with a gasp and a whoop. South was only a few yards away! "Faster girl!" she yelped, giving her another kick.

The mare broke into a gallop.

17

"You know, John South wasn't all bad or he woulda shot me off the horse," said Mashell. The entire Good News Club was clustered around her in the Gordon Brown meeting room, hanging on every word she said. And she was loving every minute of it.

Carlos chuckled. "I wish I could've seen him chasing you. The helicopter guy said he was running full blast, you know? As if he could catch a galloping horse." He laughed harder and the others joined him. "For funny!"

"I'm glad he finally gave up," said Anna.

Felipe shook his head. "He was *so stupid* to think he could get away in the first place. They had half an army after him! *I* wish I could have seen it when those helicopter guys landed the thing and jumped out and got him." He punched an imaginary drug smuggler with his fists.

"*You* saw it," said Carlos to Mashell. "What was the fight like? Did they do a lot of shooting?"

She gave him a sideways glare. "You kiddin'? I was too busy keepin' my *hide* in one piece to bother 'bout somebody else's fight! I figured out how to get a horse to move, but I didn't have a *clue* how to get it to stop! I finally dropped the reins and she stopped by herself. An' I was *glad* to let 'er do it!"

Carlos looked at her with envy. "And then you got to ride in a helicopter. *Lucky!*"

Mashell gave him a self-satisfied grin.

"I'm really glad it all worked out," said the newest Good News Club member. "I thought I'd ruined my whole life and yours, too." Bronce gave his head a relieved shake. Then he looked at Carlos and said, "You know, I did what you said. I asked Jesus to make me a Christian. I asked Him to forgive me for doin' wrong an' I told Him I wanted *Him* to run my life 'cause I *sure* wasn't doin' any good at it!"

The oldest Good News Club kids cheered because they knew exactly what he was talking about. The younger ones cheered because they heard the others doing it.

"Did you ever have to go to jail?" Felipe asked Bronce.

"No. I'm on probation, though. I got a juvenile officer that checks up on me all the time. An' I gotta go to counseling. They already been talkin' to my family. The *best* news is, I ain't gonna have to leave my home or nothin'.

The kids cheered again, and Bronce went on. "I mean it ain't my mom's fault I smuggled drugs. I made that brilliant choice *myself.*"

At that moment, the doors to the meeting room burst open and four anxious adults hurried in. Mrs. Peterson, Mrs. Joyce, Miss Lindstrom and Stan.

"I was afraid the kids would be standing at the door waiting for us," Mrs. Peterson was saying. "They wouldn't have left already...."

She paused and stared at the thirty or so children blankly. All the adults seemed utterly stunned to see them sitting calmly in their seats.

"How did you get *in?*" spluttered Mrs. Joyce.

"Maintenance man," answered Mashell.

Mrs. Peterson beamed at them. "And *look* at you, all in your places and being quiet! I'm *impressed!*"

As subtly as she could, Mashell gave Anna a look that said, *What does she think we are? Kindergartners?*

The teachers wasted no time getting the meeting started. Miss Lindstrom played the guitar and they sang several songs that everyone knew. Then the kids, with Stan and Miss Lindstrom's help, taught Mrs. Peterson and Mrs. Joyce—the two teachers who'd stayed behind in Los Angeles—a praise song they'd learned at camp.

Before she began the Bible story, Mrs. Peterson stood with her I've-got-a-surprise-for-you look on her face. The kids exchanged bright glances as Stan walked to the front of the room carrying a package wrapped in bright paper and tied with a curly ribbon.

Whose birthday? wondered Mashell.

The young man smiled at the group and looked excited, like a child about to blurt out a huge secret. "Before we go on, I have a gift for someone special in this room. We have a young lady here who was in a terrible, dangerous situation. But instead of thinking only of herself, she thought of somebody else's needs."

His eyes fell on Mashell. She was sitting in the back row and the entire group turned and stared at her. She felt her face grow hot and her hands start to tremble. *What in the world?*

Stan went on. "Most of you know that the drug smuggler, John South, held both Mashell and Felipe hostage. But some of you *might* not know that she carried in her pocket a transmitter that gave off signals. The Yosemite National Park rangers were able to locate South's hideout because of those signals."

He fumbled with the package. "However, there reached a point where South took her with him and left Felipe behind, alone in the wilderness and lost. Mashell, worried that no one would ever find him, dropped the transmitter in some nearby bushes so the rangers would be led right to where Felipe was. She went on with South, knowing the rangers would no longer have a guaranteed way to find her."

The kids broke into applause. Felipe gave her a grin that made her eyes grow wet. Stan spoke to her directly. "You know, Mashell, there's a Bible verse that talks about what you did." He glanced at Miss Lindstrom, who apparently was supposed to stand up and read from the Bible on her lap. But she was busy wiping her eyes with a tissue. In the middle of blowing her nose, she suddenly realized the entire group was waiting for her. She sprang up and the Bible nearly toppled to the floor. *"Oh!"* she cried, making a frantic catch. She hurried to open it, realized she had the book upside down and started page-flipping madly.

Mashell giggled softly, glad that *something* was keeping her from crying. "John fifteen, verse thirteen," said Mrs. Lindstrom. "This is Jesus speaking: 'Greater love has no one than this, that he lay down his life for his friends.' " She caught Mashell's eye. "Jesus did that for us, but He also wants us to do that for each other. Mashell, put *she* and *her* in place of he and his, and that verse describes exactly what you did. 'Greater love has no one than this, that she lay down her life for—' "

She began to cry too hard to talk. "Boys and girls, finish the verse!" blurted out Mrs. Joyce.

"Her friends!" yelled the kids.

"So," continued Stan, "on behalf of the rangers of Yosemite National Park, the staff of Pine Lake Bible Camp and your Good News Club teachers, I'd like to present you with *this.*"

He thrust the package toward her and she walked up front to receive it in a daze of joyful embarrassment. It took her awhile to tear away the wrapping and reveal a white cardboard box. The kids were starting to fidget in eager impatience. Every eye was glued on her as she fought to break the tape they'd sealed it shut with.

At last! One end popped open. She tilted the box and the something inside slid against her palm. Hard, cool metal with smooth sides and corners that let her fingers run easily along them. She pulled it all the way out and stared open-mouthed at a shiny silver transmitter box exactly like the one she'd carried in her pocket. Only this one was hollow and it had already familiar words engraved on its side: John 15:13 written out with *she* and *her* in parentheses after he and his.

She rotated it in her hand and saw etched on the other side, "To Mashell Robertson with love, from her many friends at Yosemite National Park, Pine Lake Bible Camp and the Gordon Brown Good News Club."

The kids could no longer stand it. "Show us what it *is!* Read what it *says!*" they yelled. Mashell held it up for them to see, but someone else would have to read it. She didn't have enough voice.

Stan read its words aloud, then brought the token transmitter box to each table so the kids could read it and touch it and run their fingers along it. As she watched them bend in toward it like springs to a magnet, she lifted up a "thank you" prayer for friends like these. She knew that any of them would do the same for her.

In any adventure they faced together.

Get a Life!

This life is short, you know—and full of trouble. That's because *we all* got a problem called sin. We do bad things that break God's laws, like lying, cheating and having mean thoughts. And because God is holy—He never does wrong—sin keeps us away from Him. That's a bad situation because the punishment for sin is to be away from God *forever*.

But there's a good side. The Bible says, "God so loved the world that he gave his one and only Son, that whoever believes in him shall not perish but have eternal life" (John 3:16). God loves *you*. That's why Jesus Christ, God's Son, died on the cross to pay for *your* sins. Three days after they buried Him, He came back to life and today He's in Heaven. That's where He wants *you* to be someday. When you trust Him to save you from your sins, He does it. Would you like Jesus to forgive you right now? Go ahead and talk to Him. You can pray something like this:

Dear God, I believe You sent Jesus to die for me. I'm sorry for the wrong things I've done. Please take away my sin and help me live a new life. Thank You for being my absolutely best, Forever Friend. Amen.

If you just trusted Jesus to save you, you have a new life inside you. This would be a great time to join a Good News Club to learn more about your new life. Call 1-800-300-4033 to find out more.

Kids everywhere

Good NEWS CLUB®

meet once a week to hear
Bible stories, sing, play games
and have a great time.

Where do they go?

Good News Club!

If you're between
5 and 12 years old and would like
to join a Good News Club near you, call:

1-800-300-4033

That's the number for USA Ministries at Child Evangelism Fellowship.
They sponsor Good News Clubs and can tell you
everything you need to know.